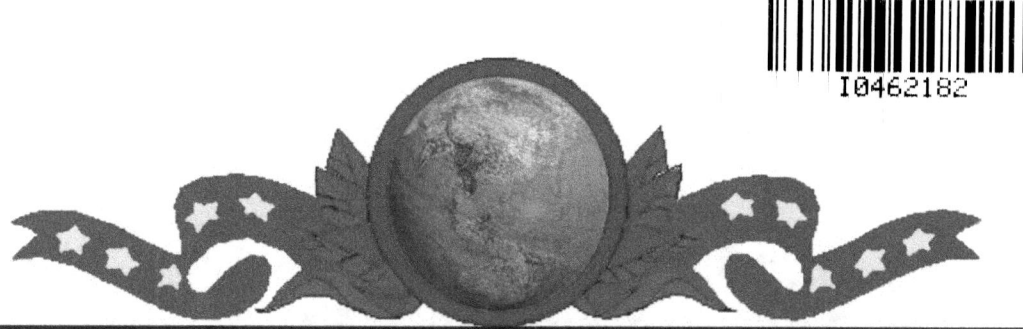

Real World
Colouring Book
For Advanced Users & Adults

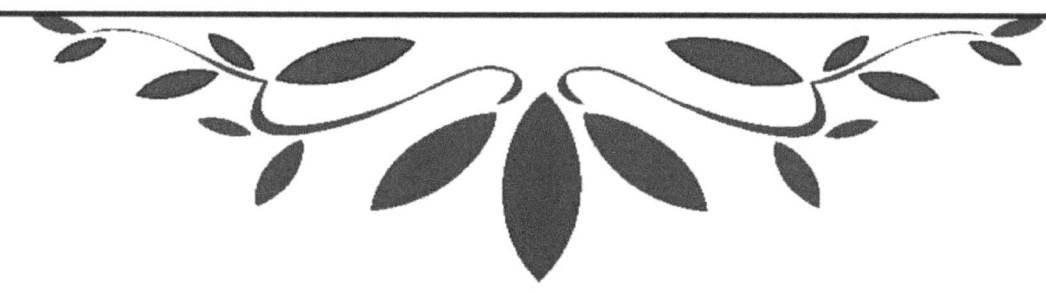

Copyright 2019 By John Boom

50 Images

Created From Real Life Photos
For You To Colour As You Please.

ISBN 978-0-359-97212-8

9 780359 972128

1884

THOMAS TAYLOR

BLACKSMITH
WHEELWRIGHT MACHINIST

NORTH

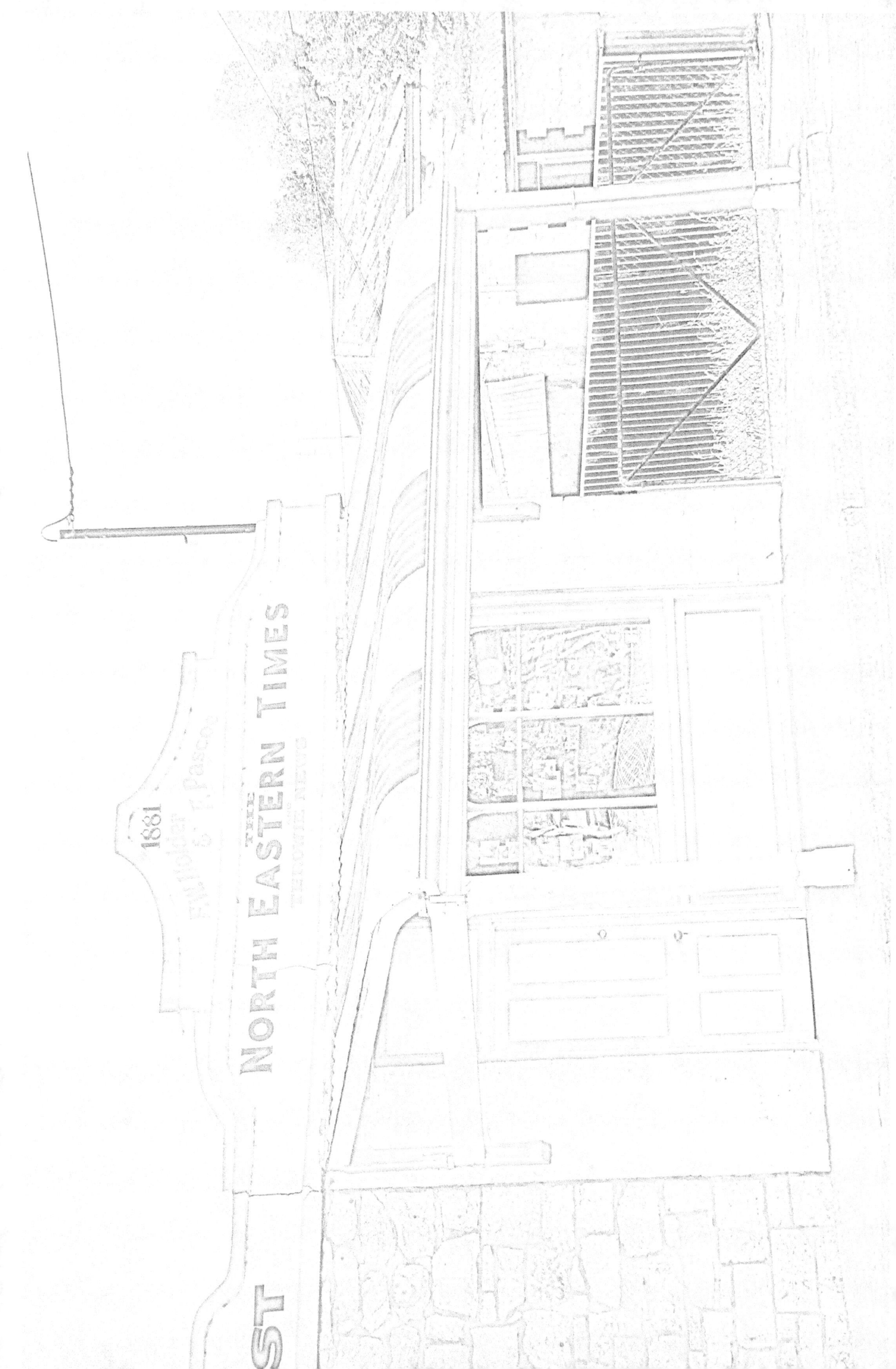

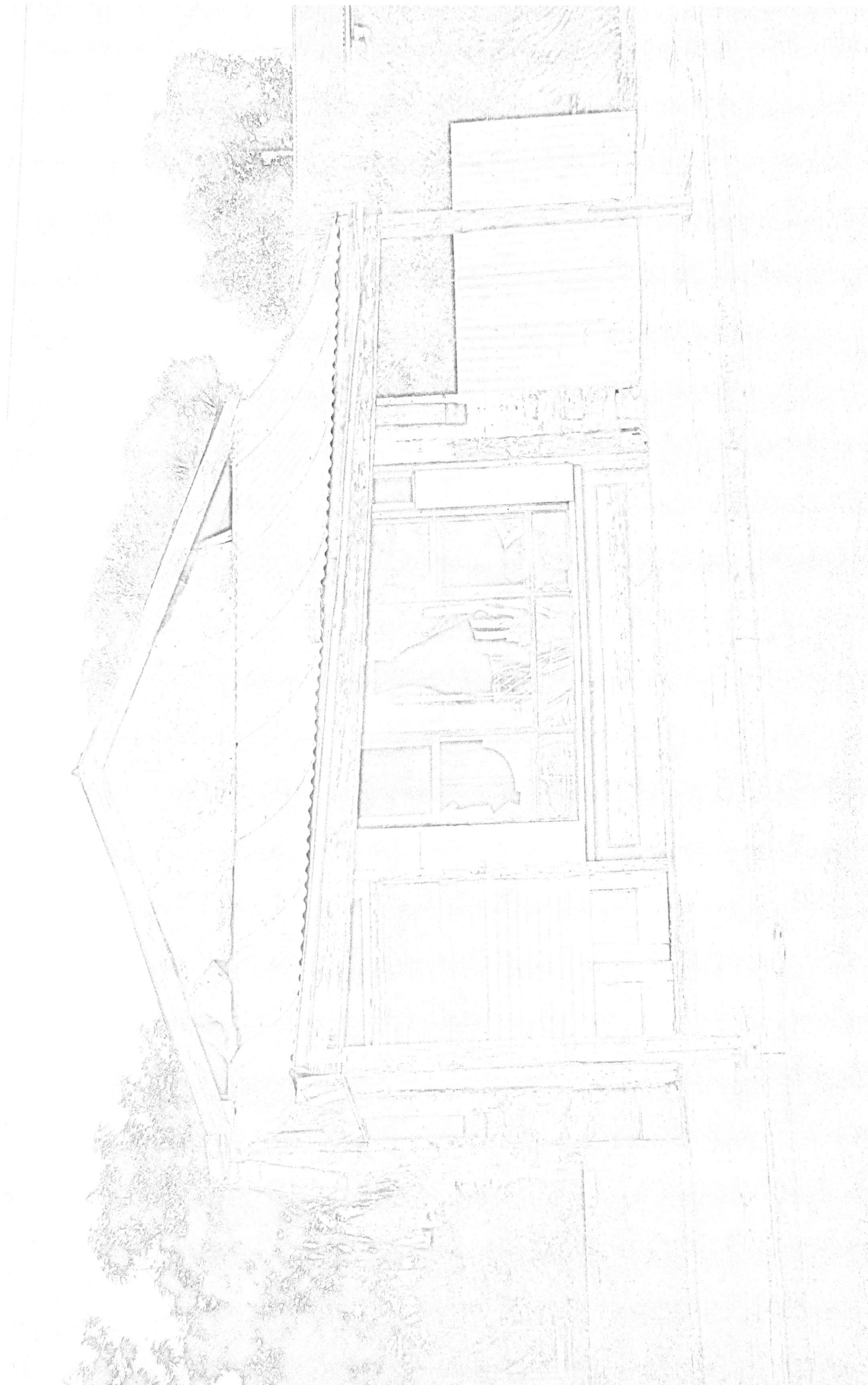

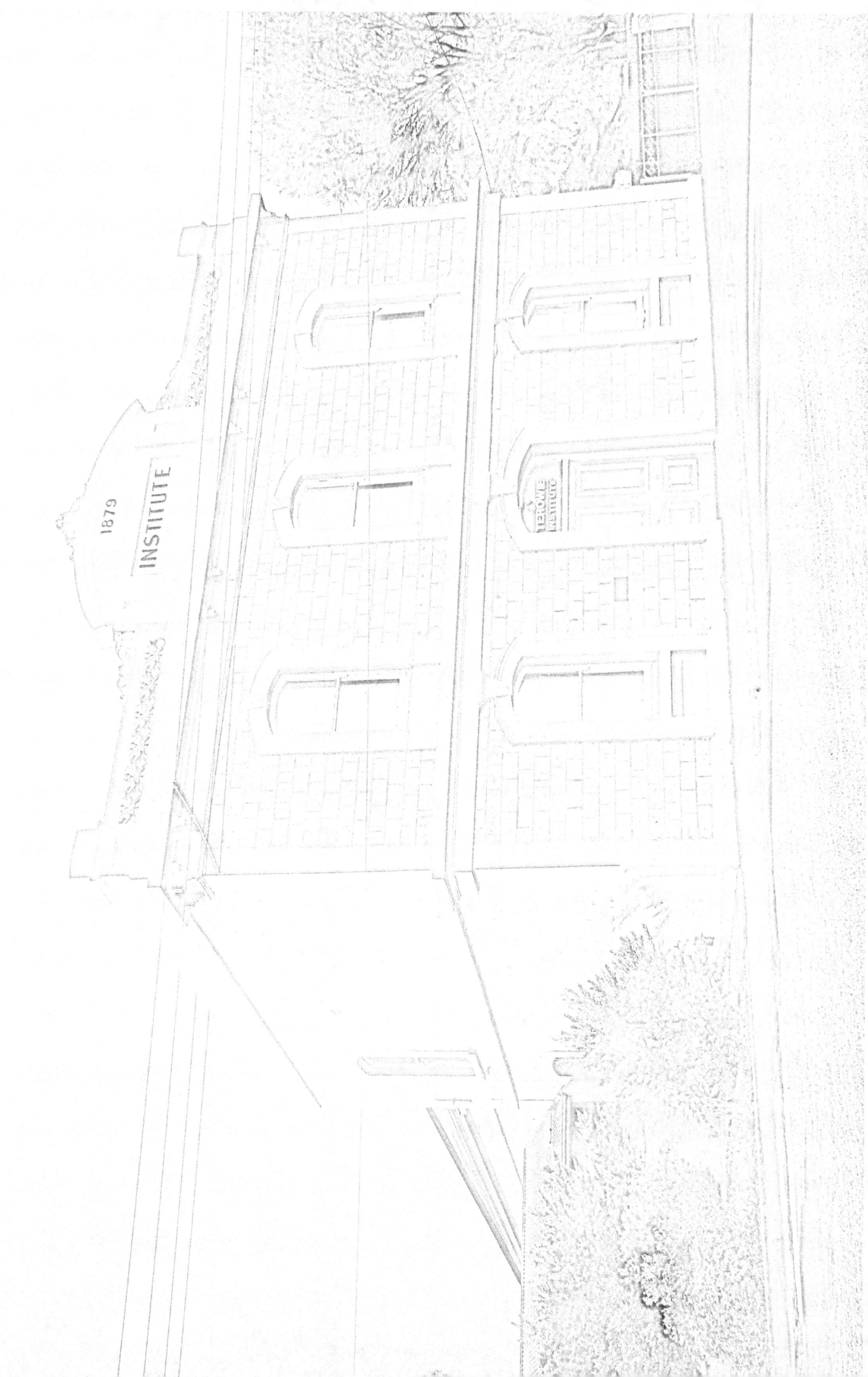

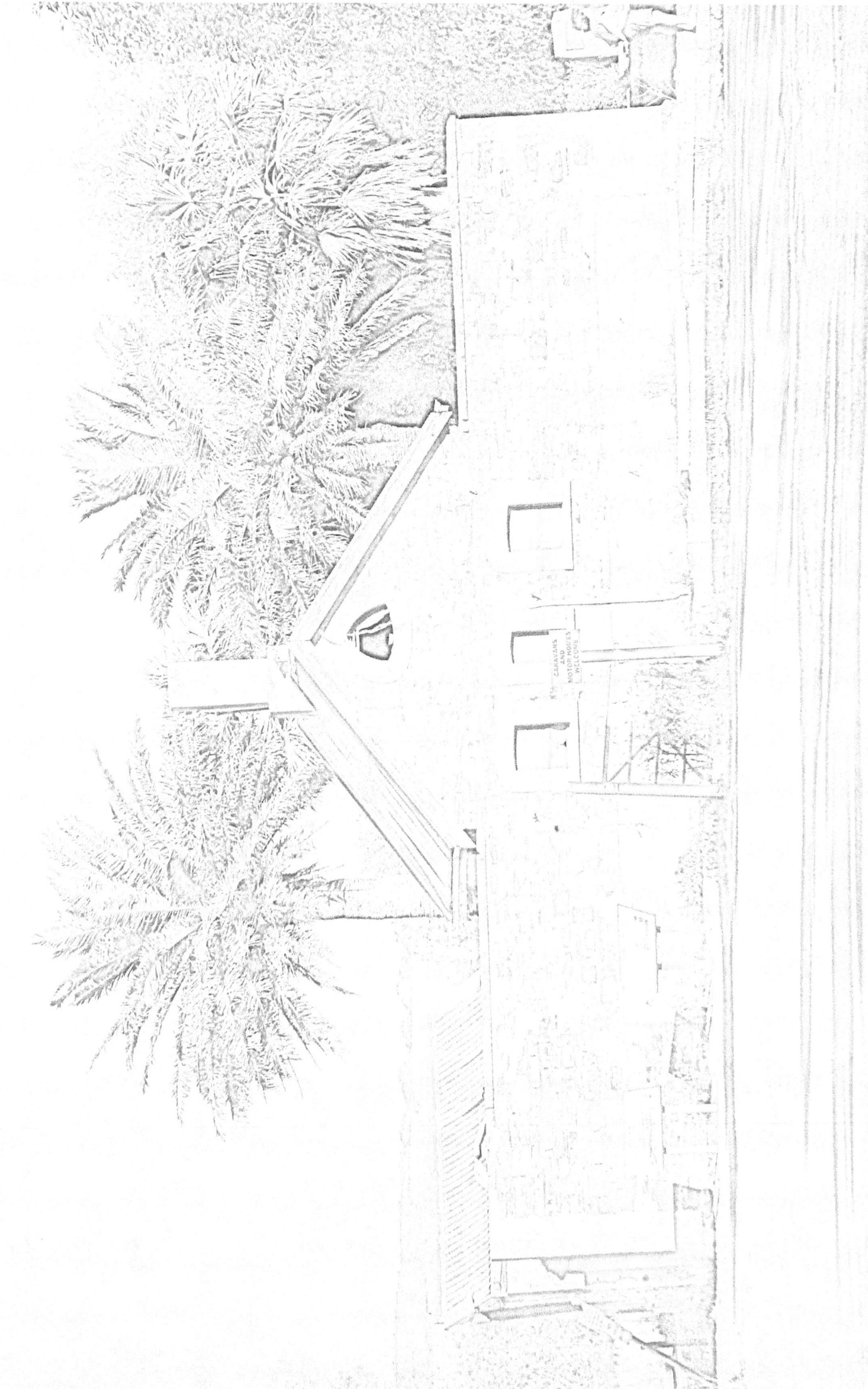

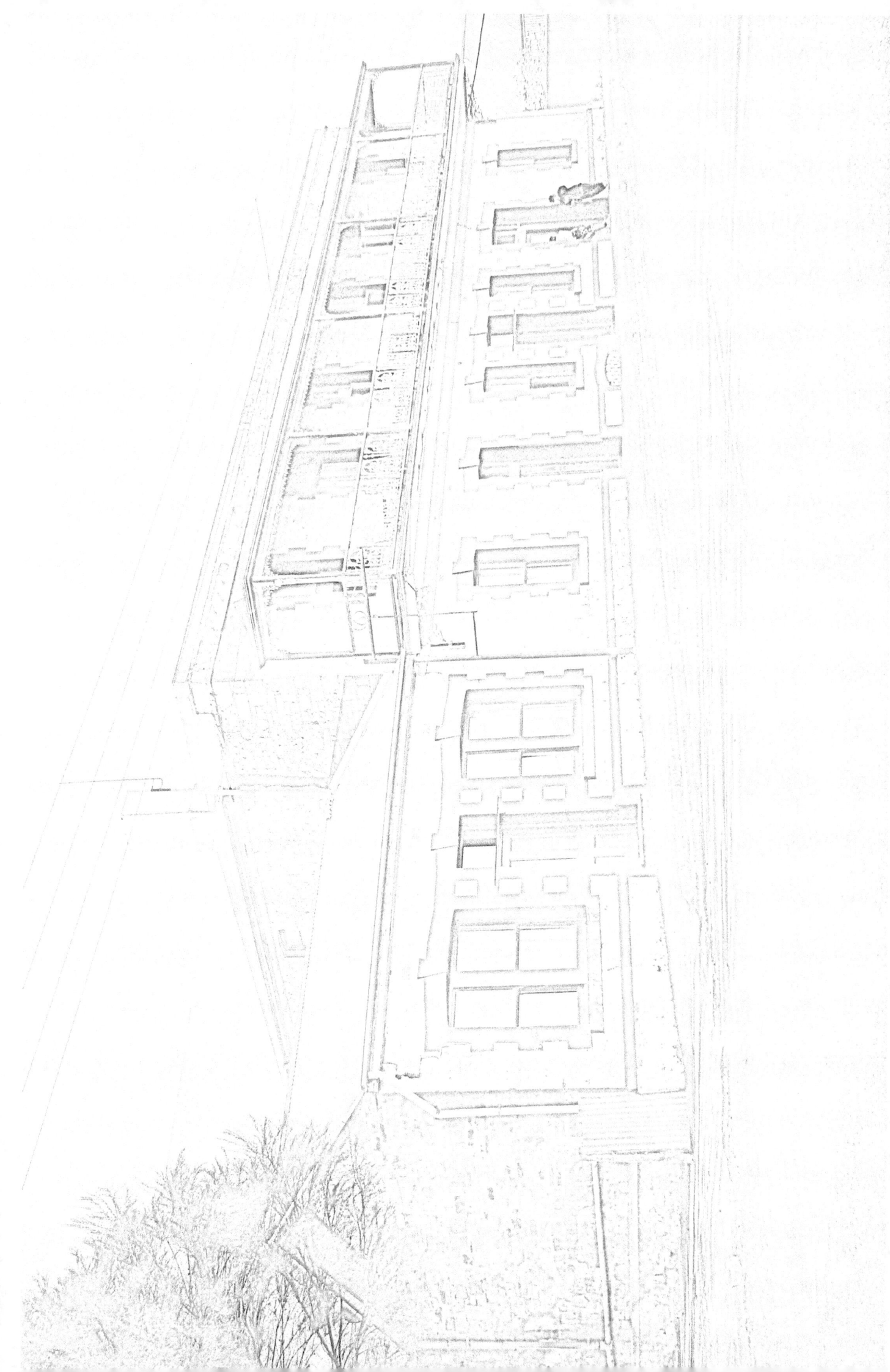

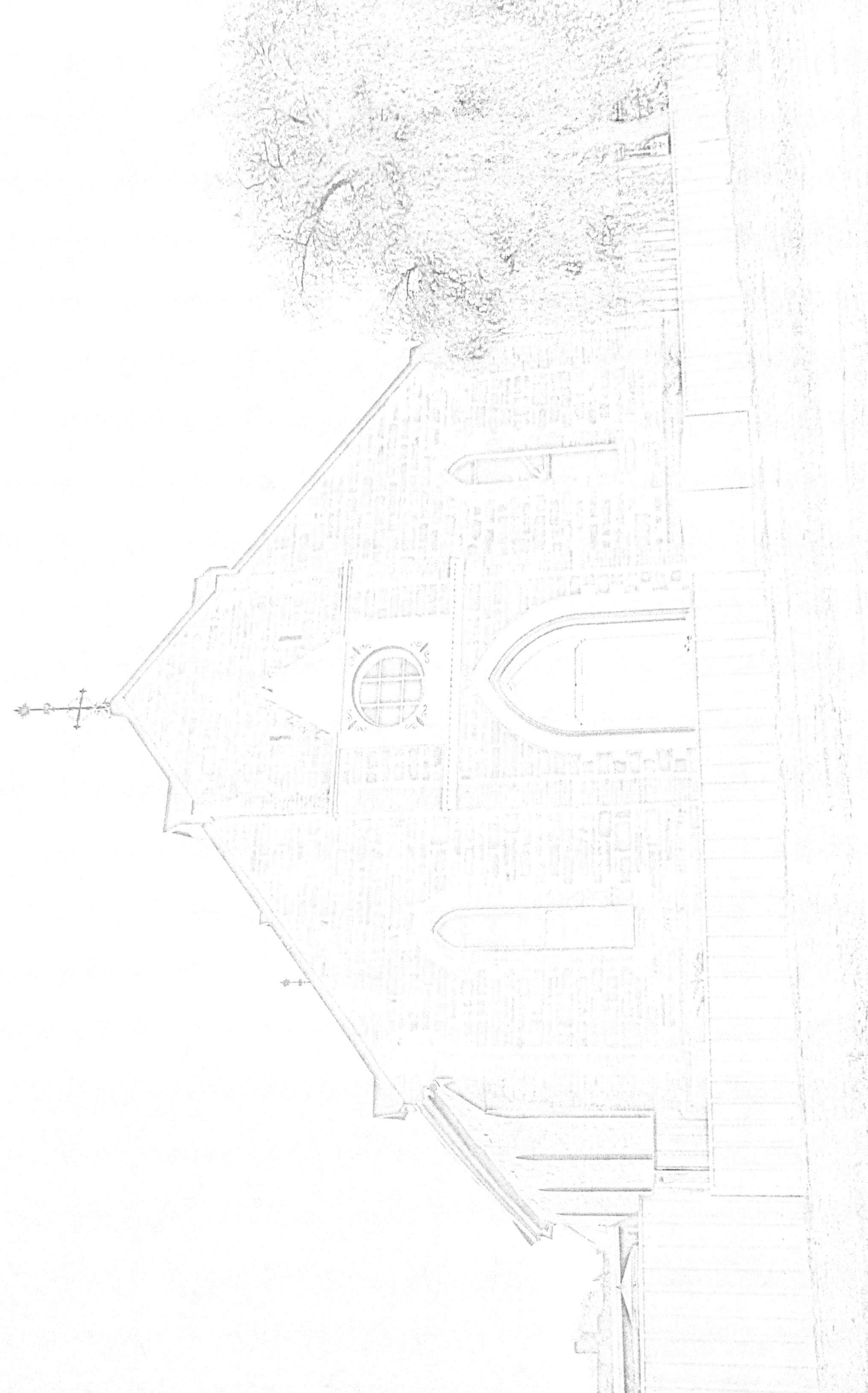

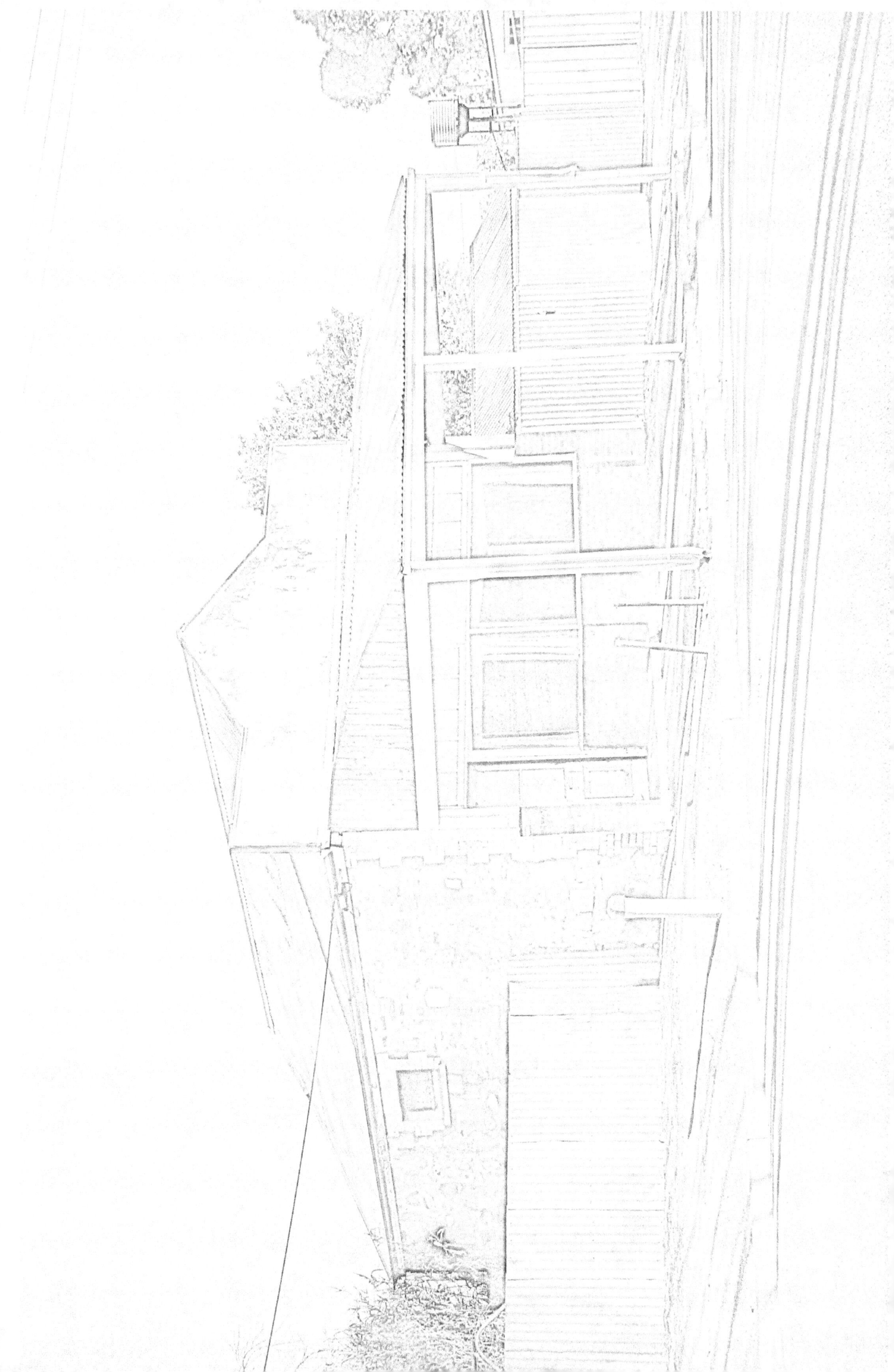

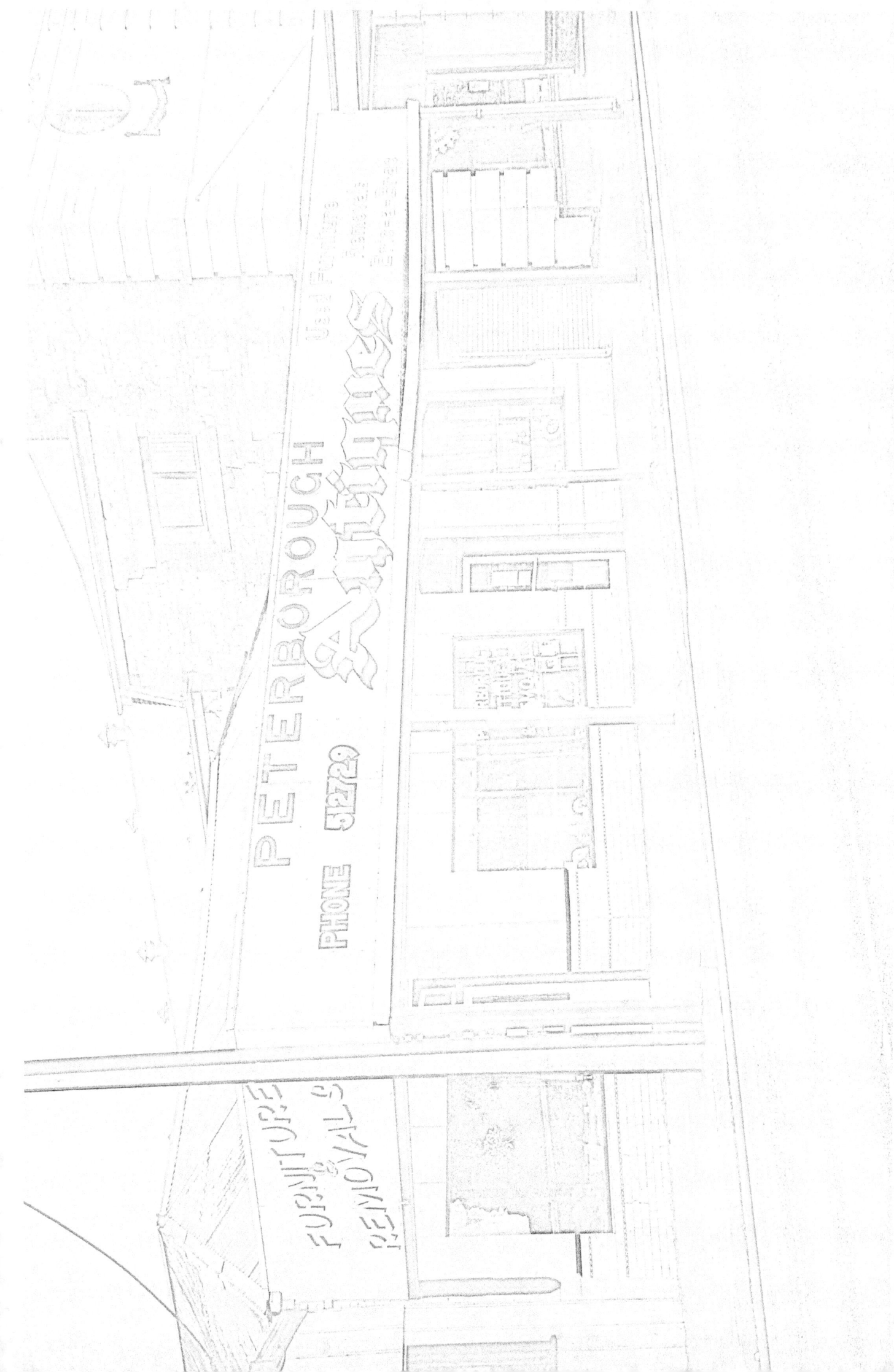

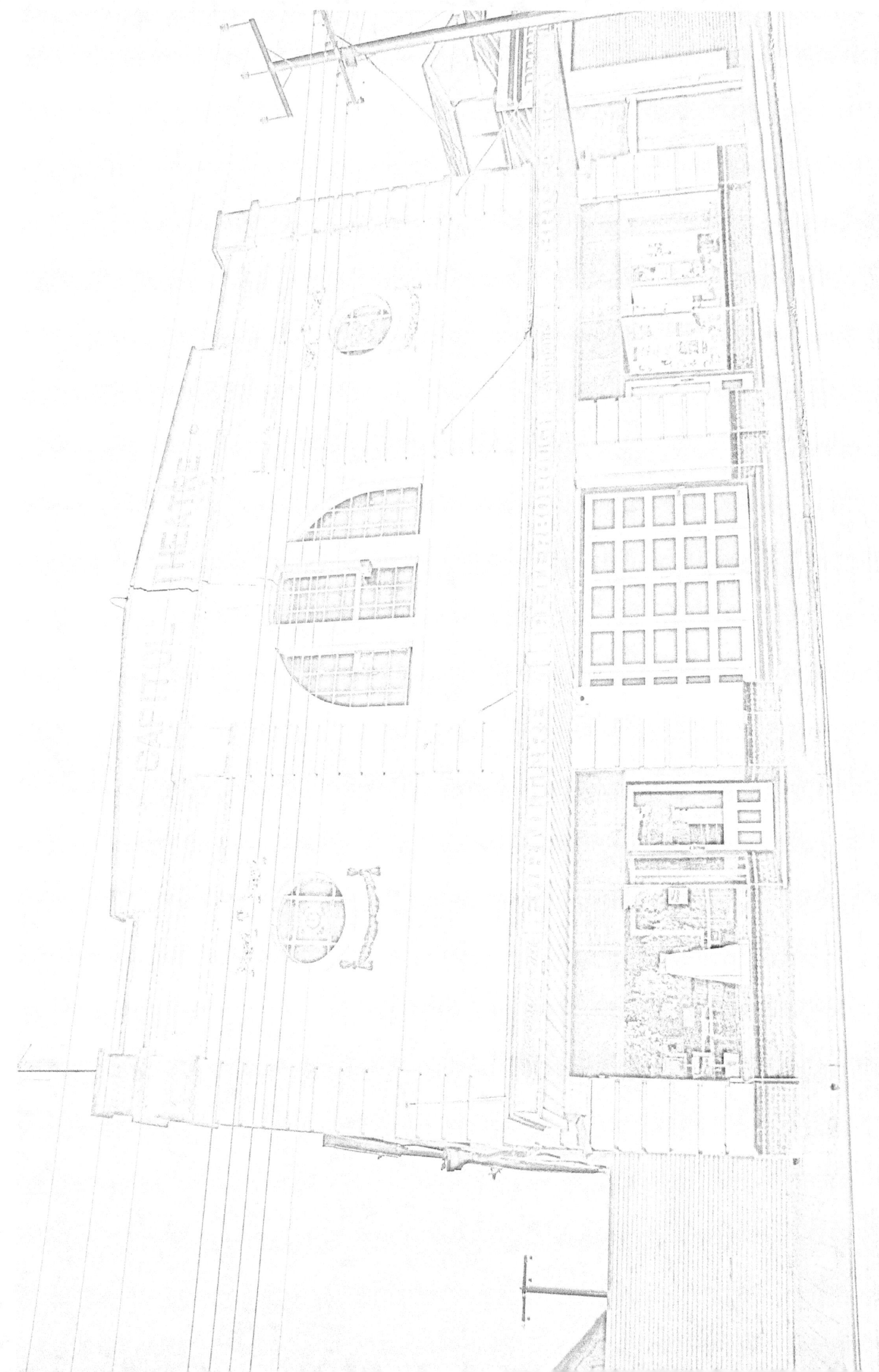

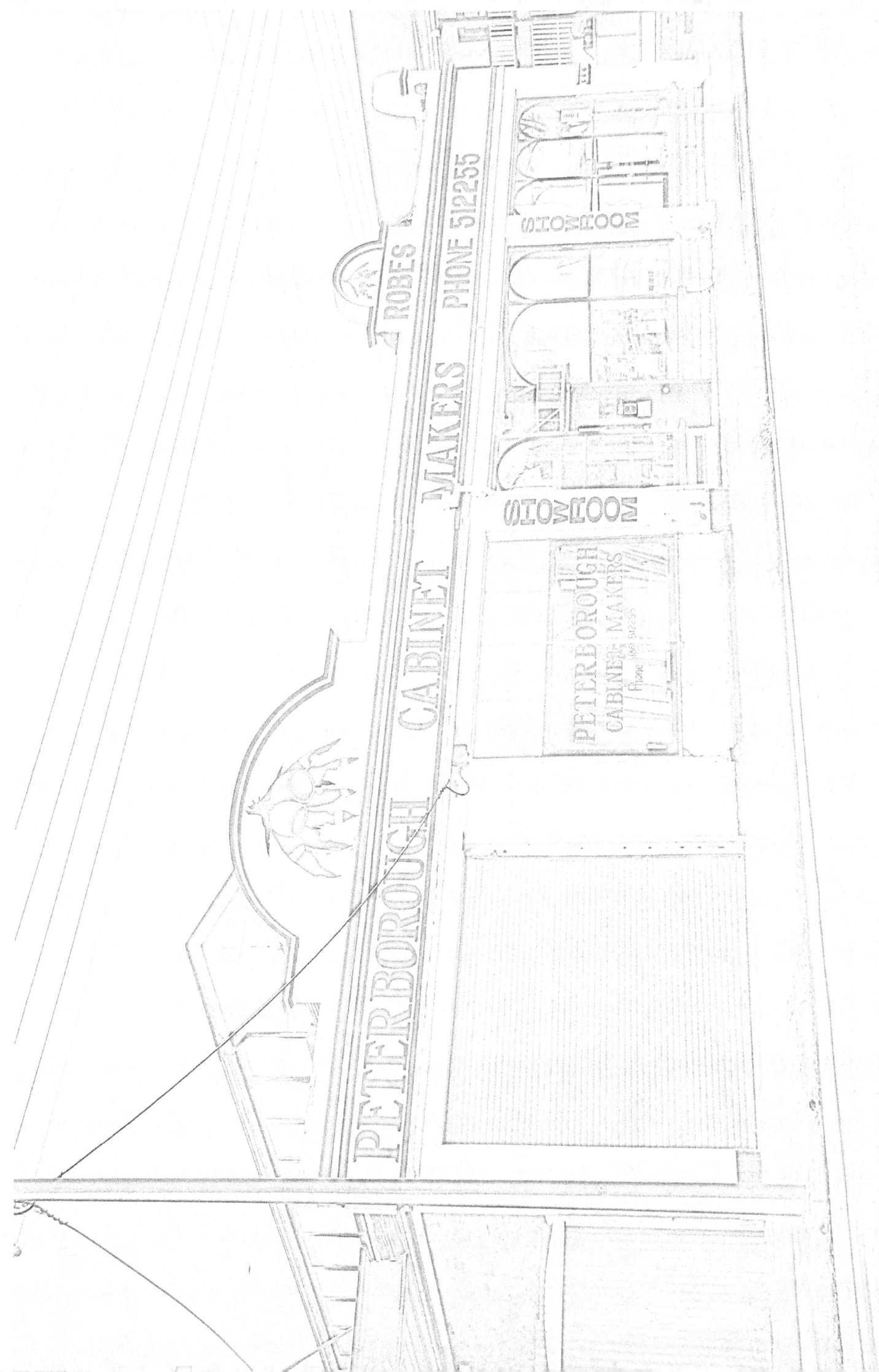

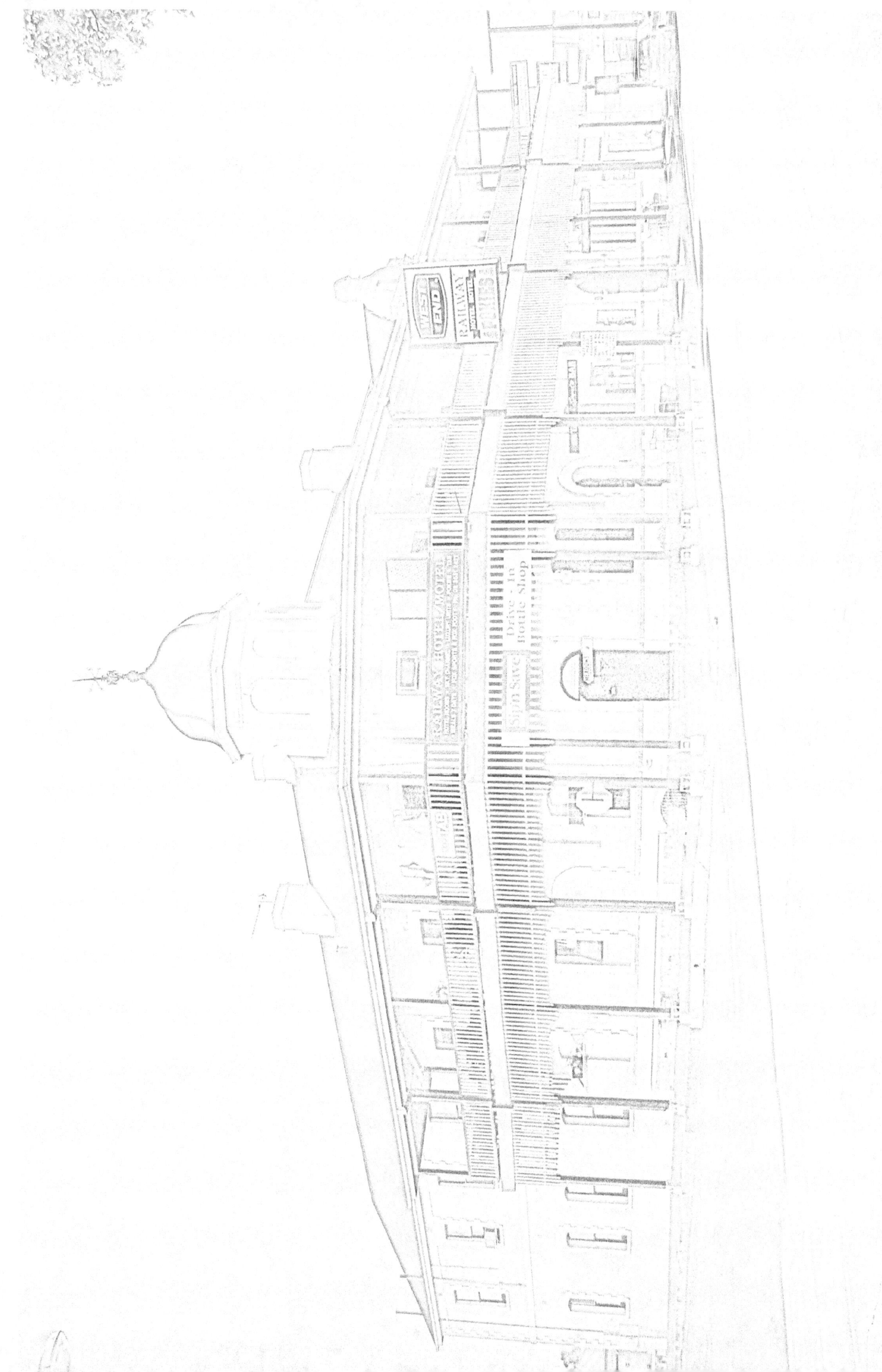

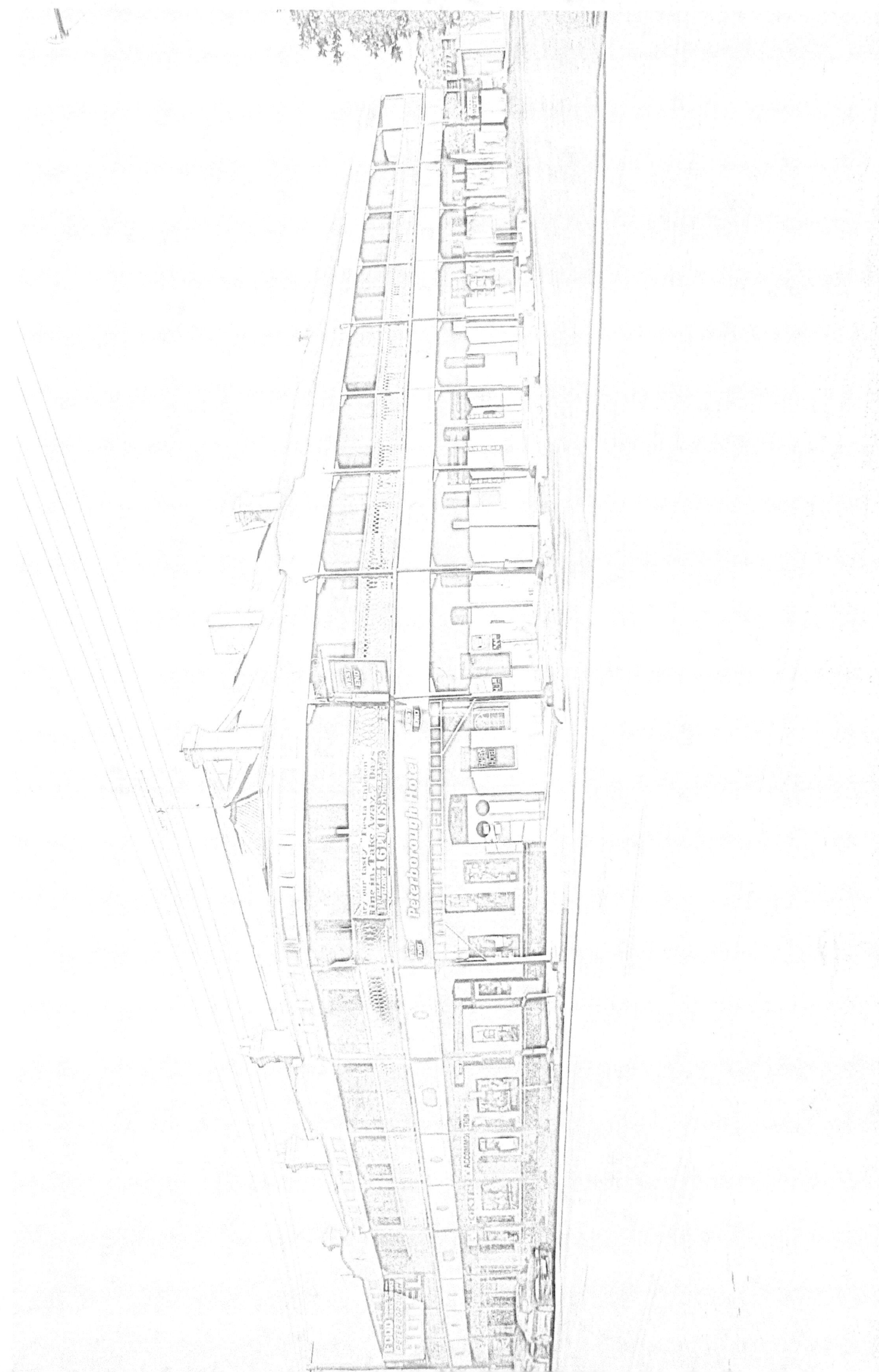

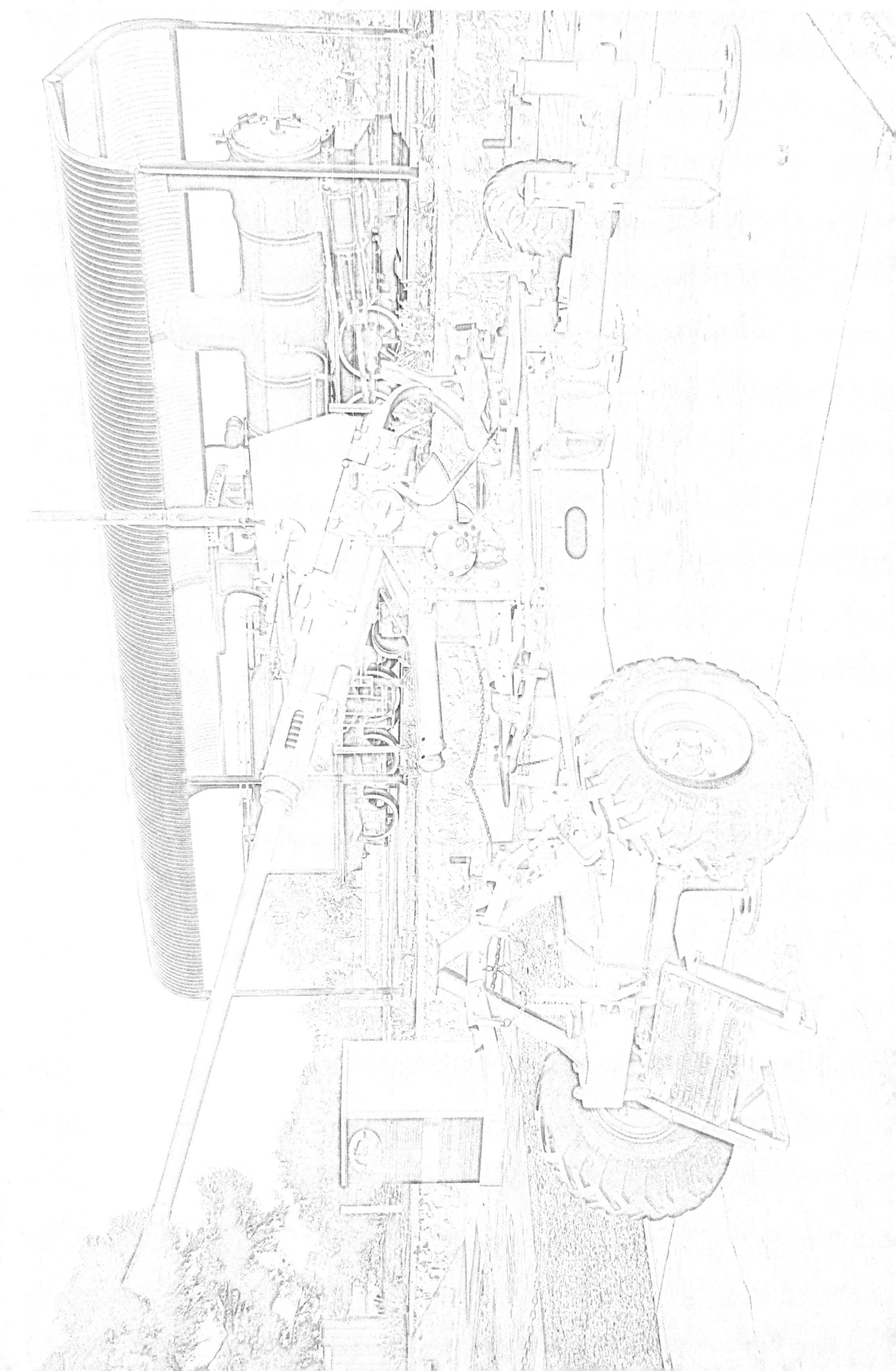

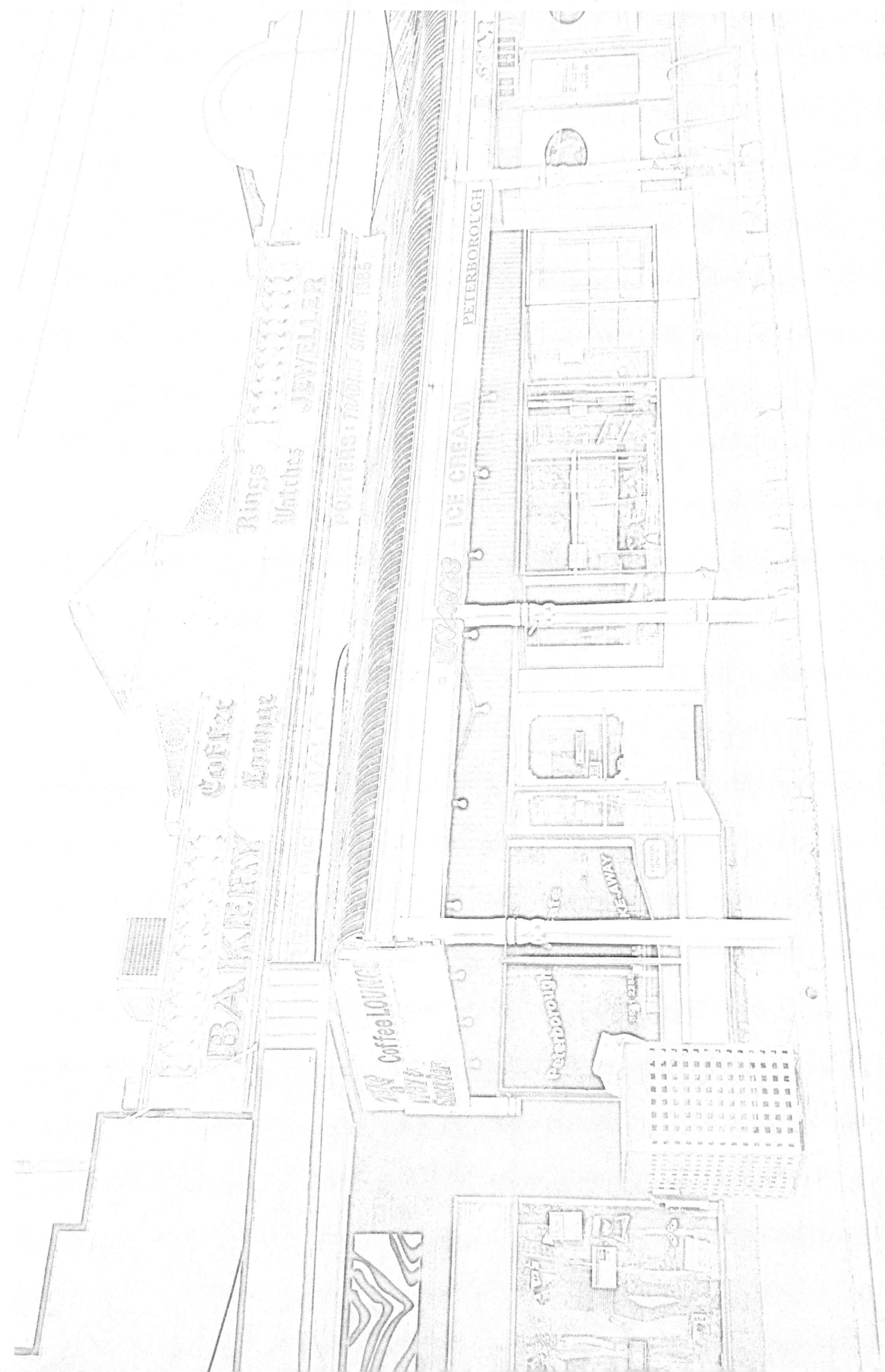

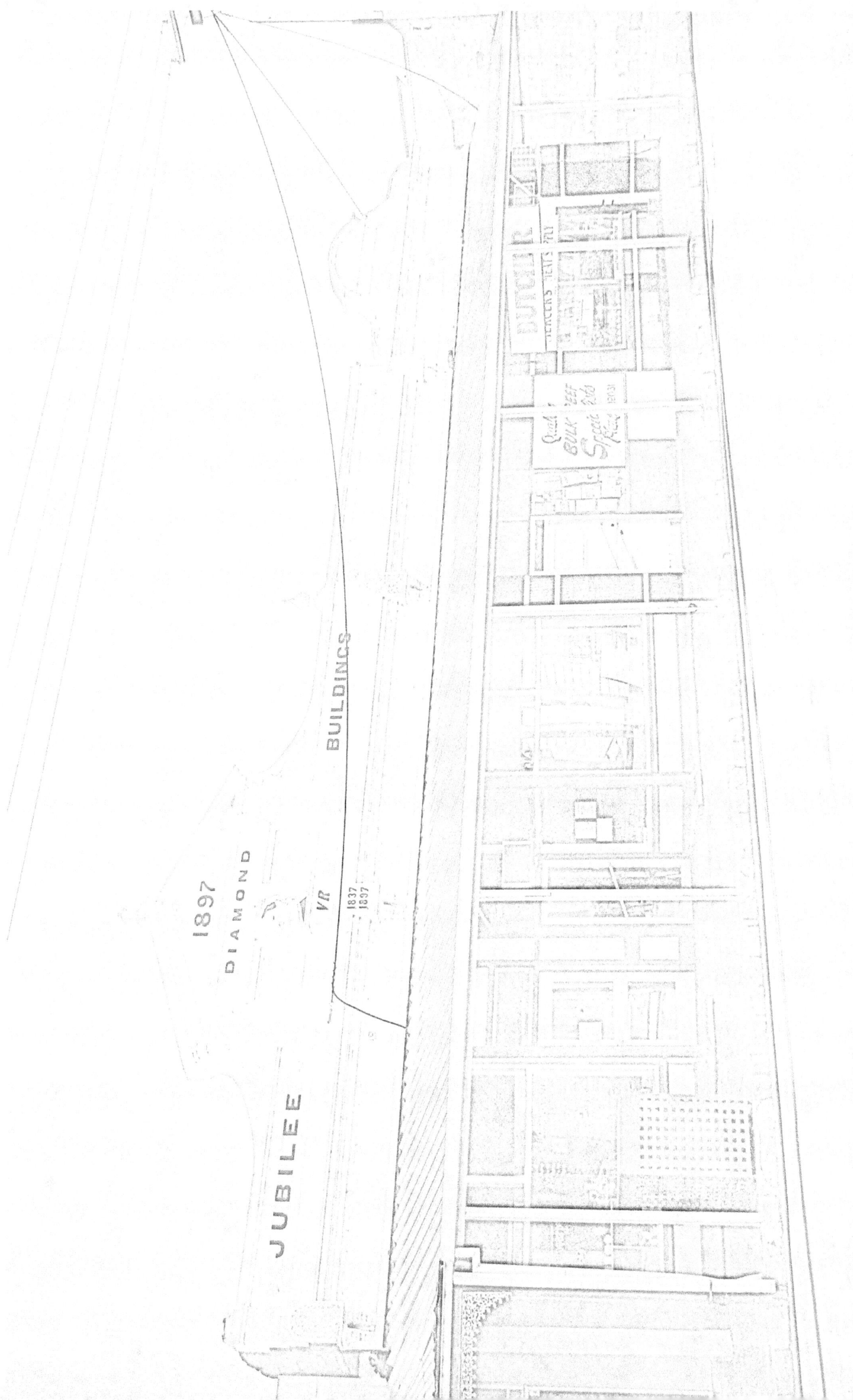

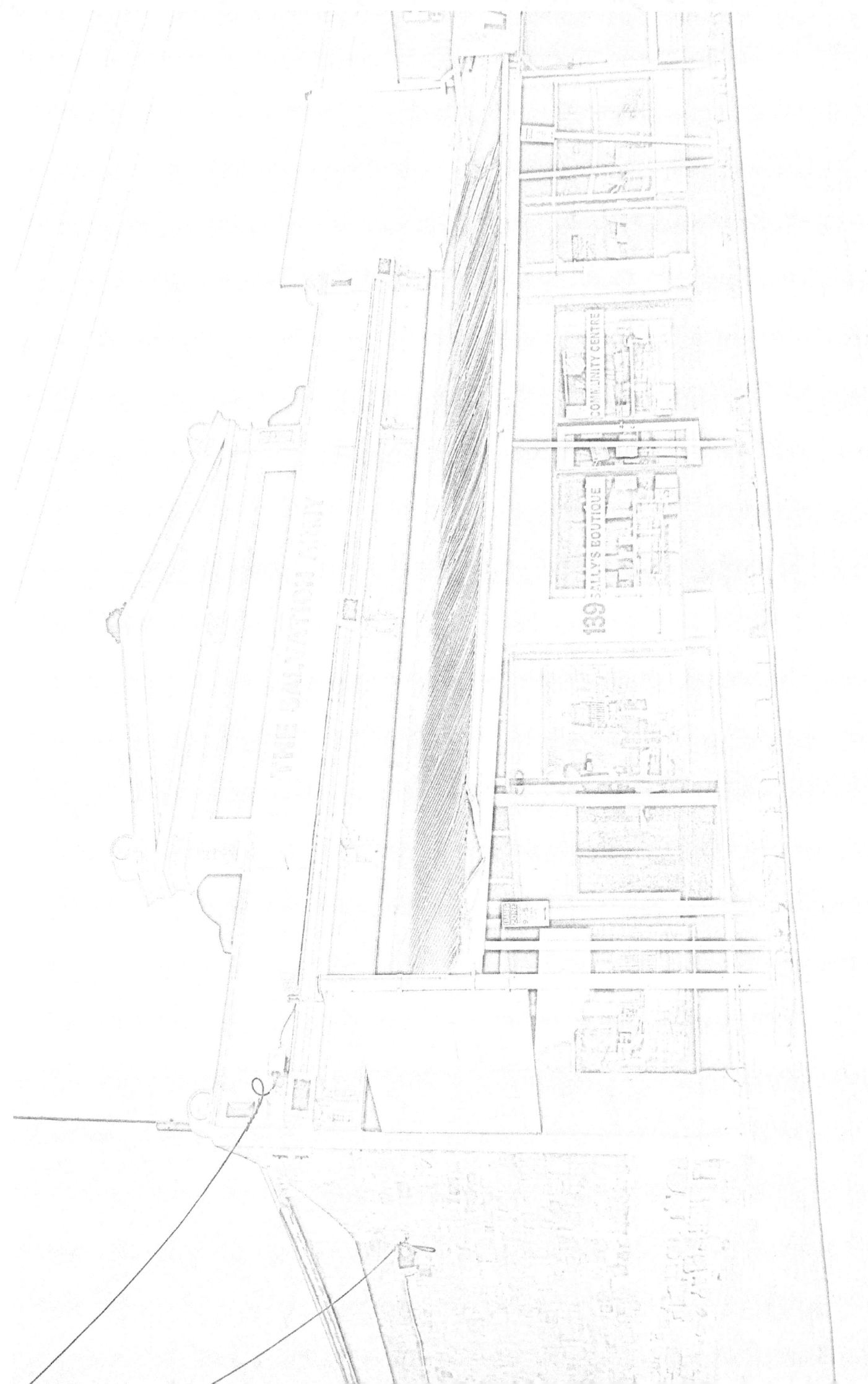

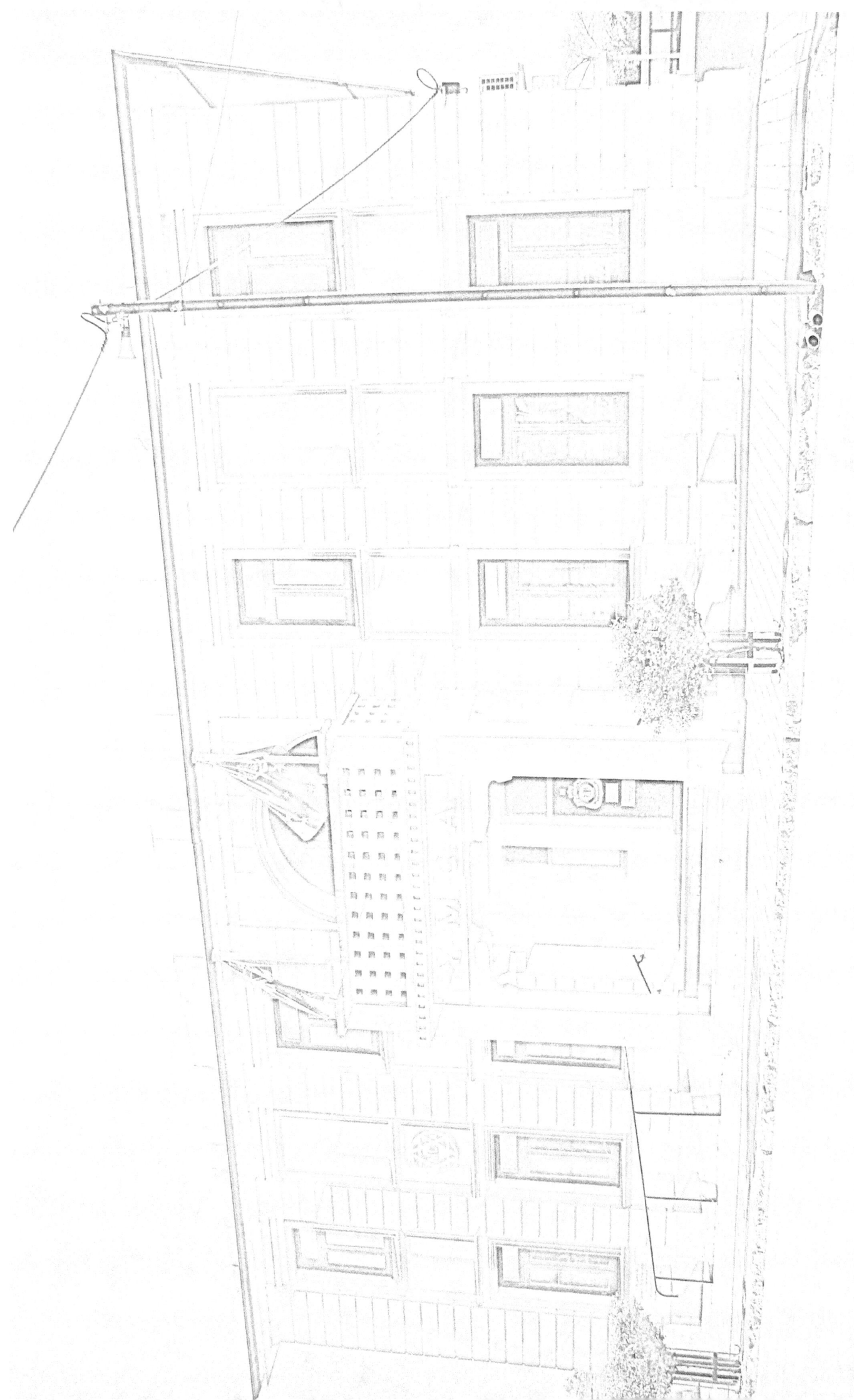

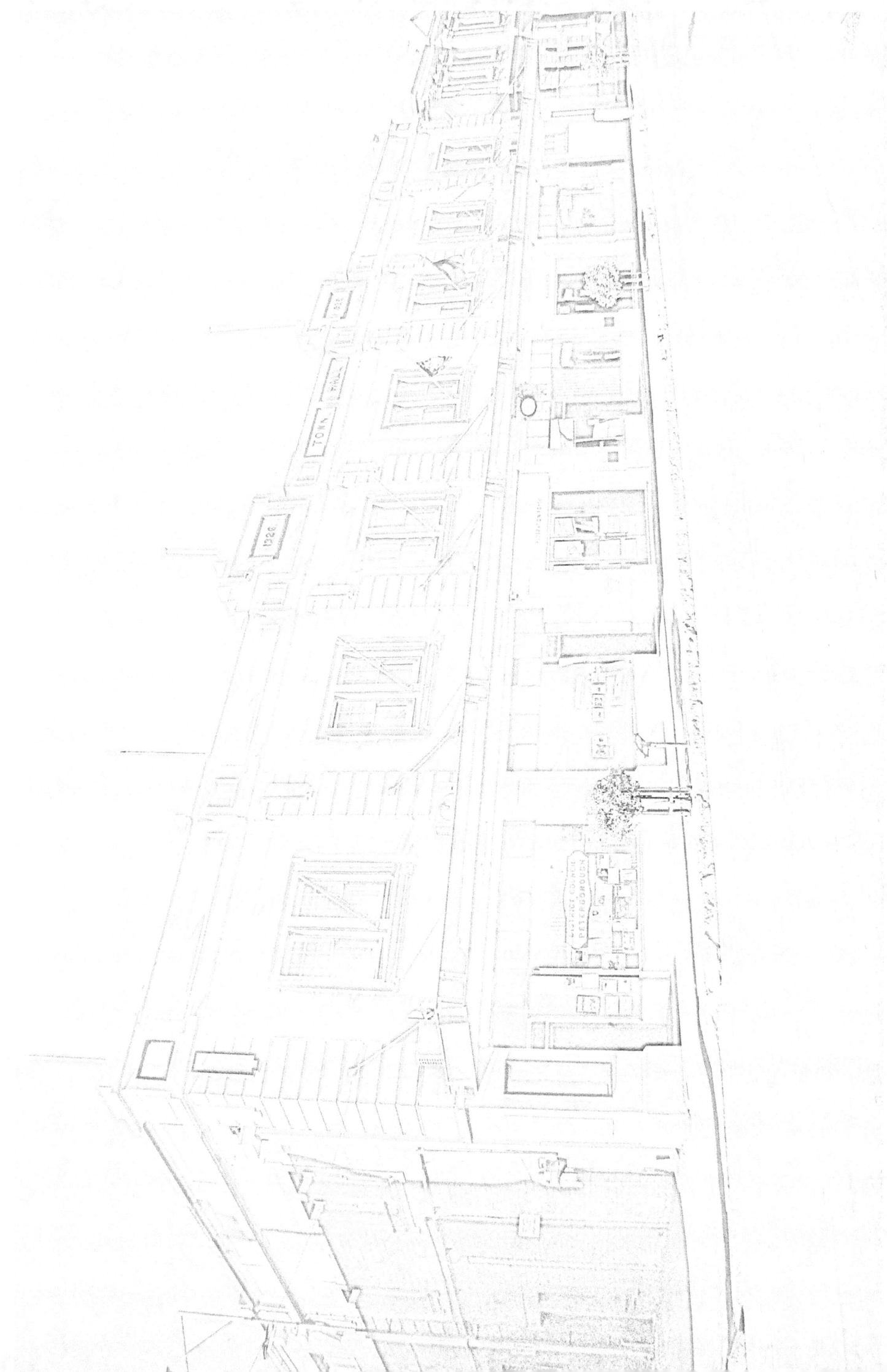

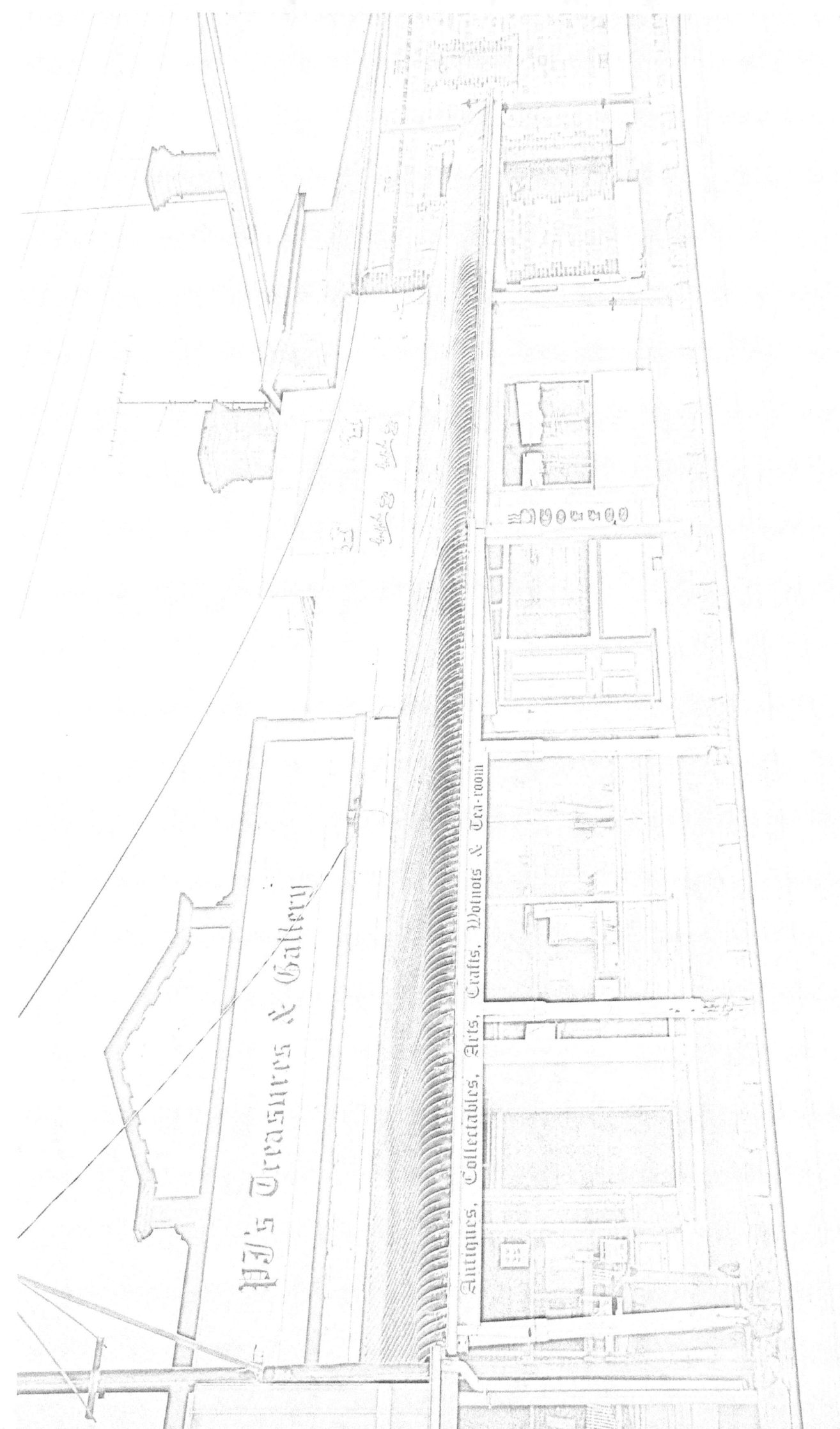

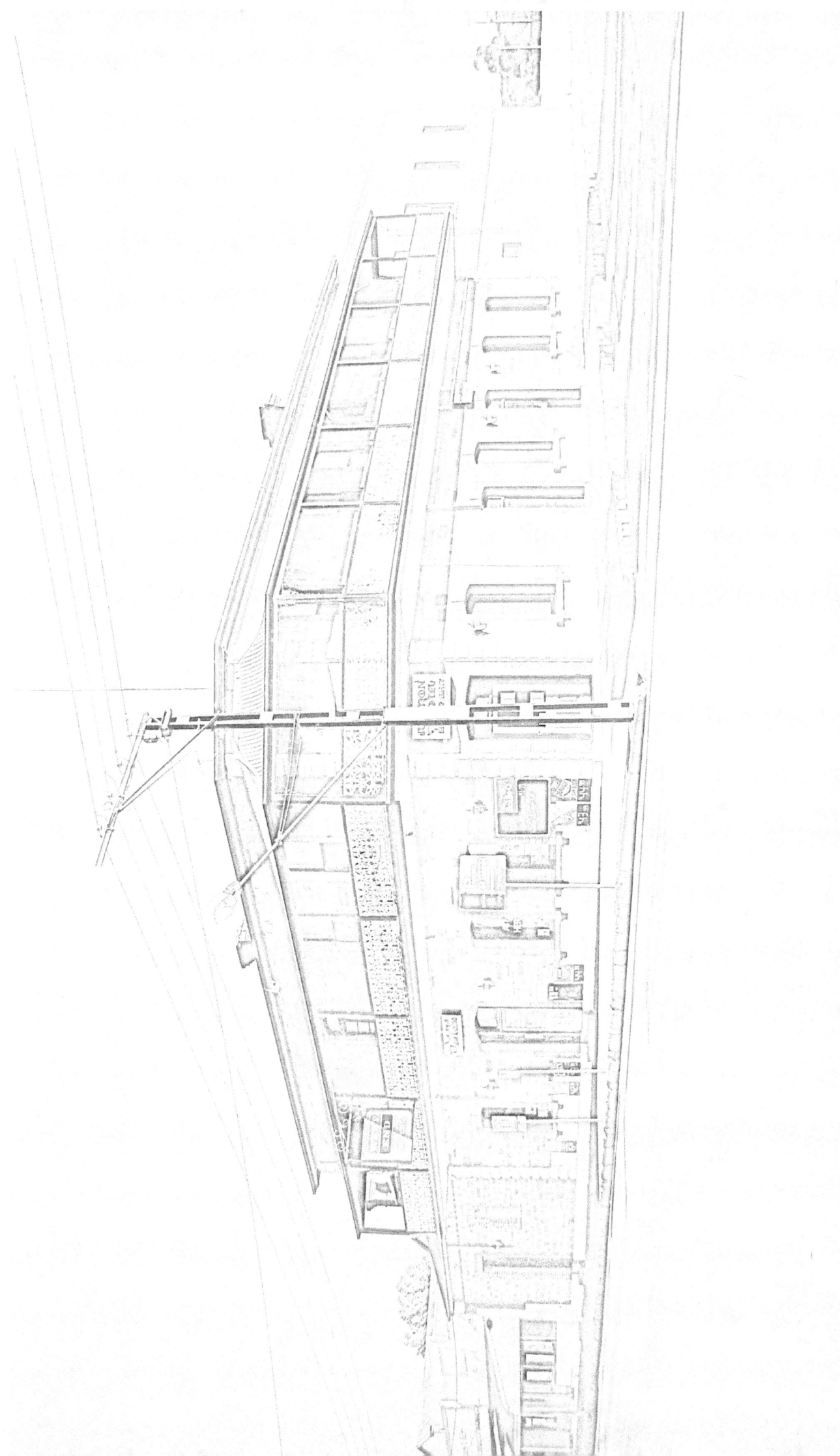

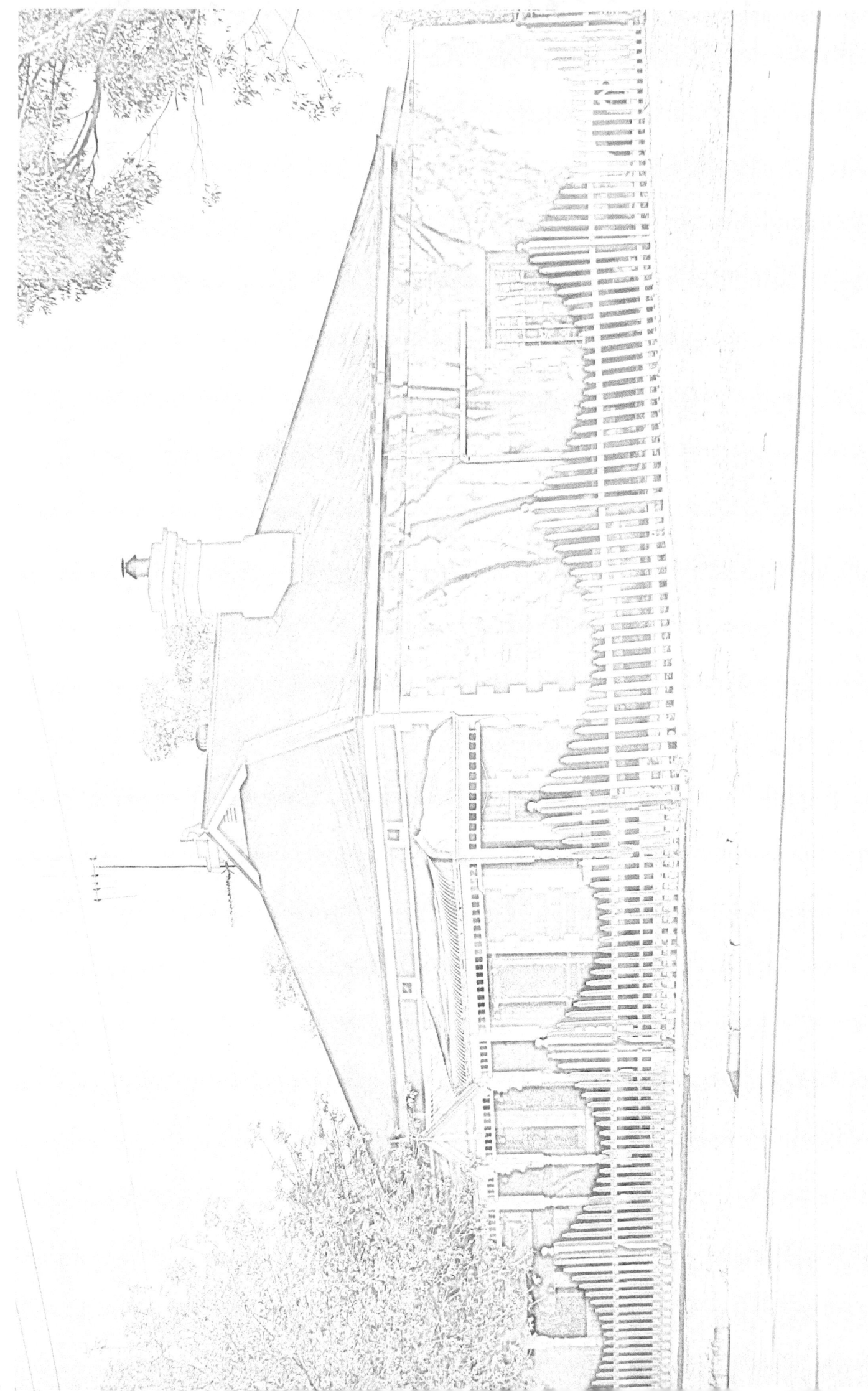

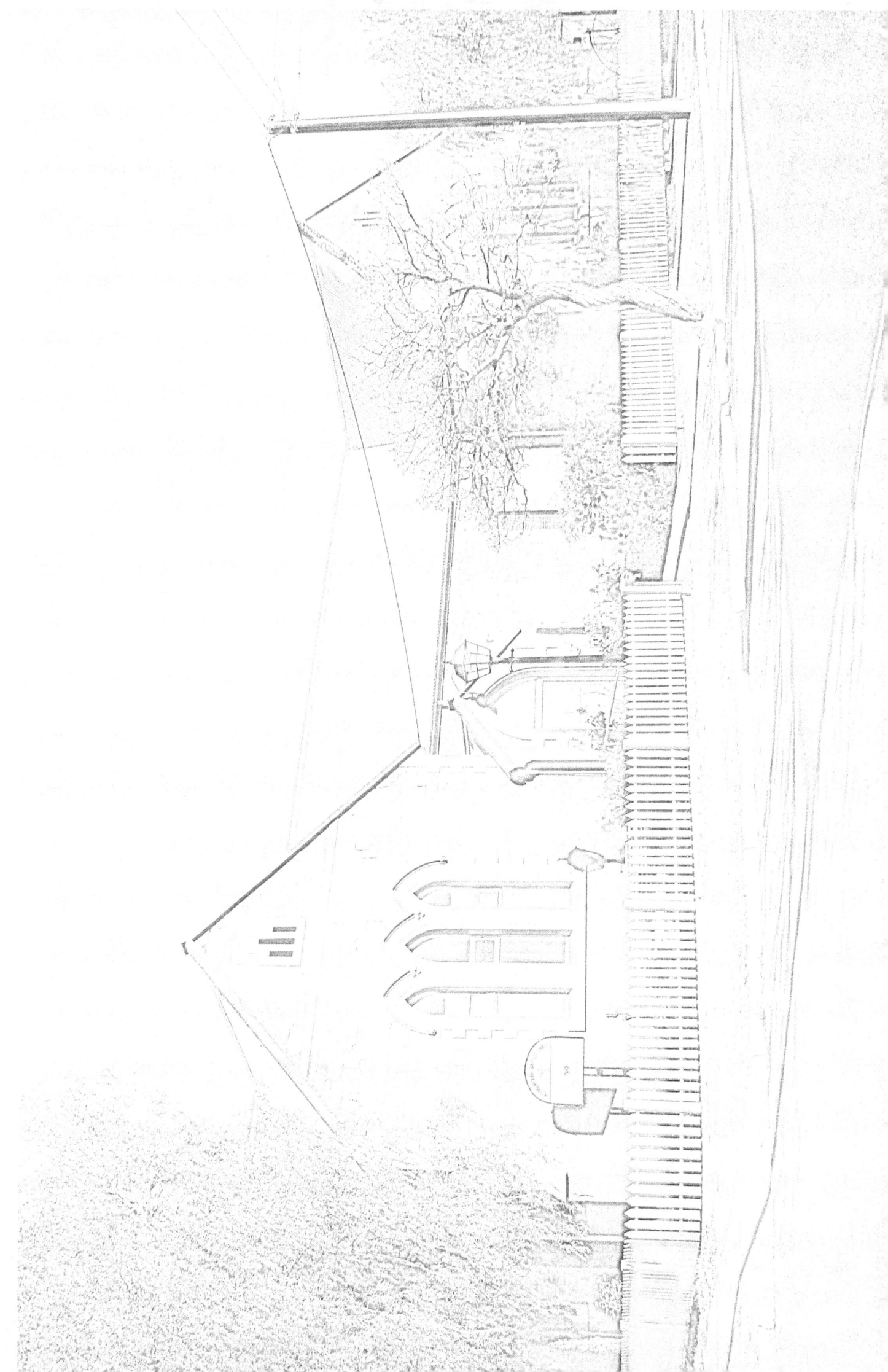

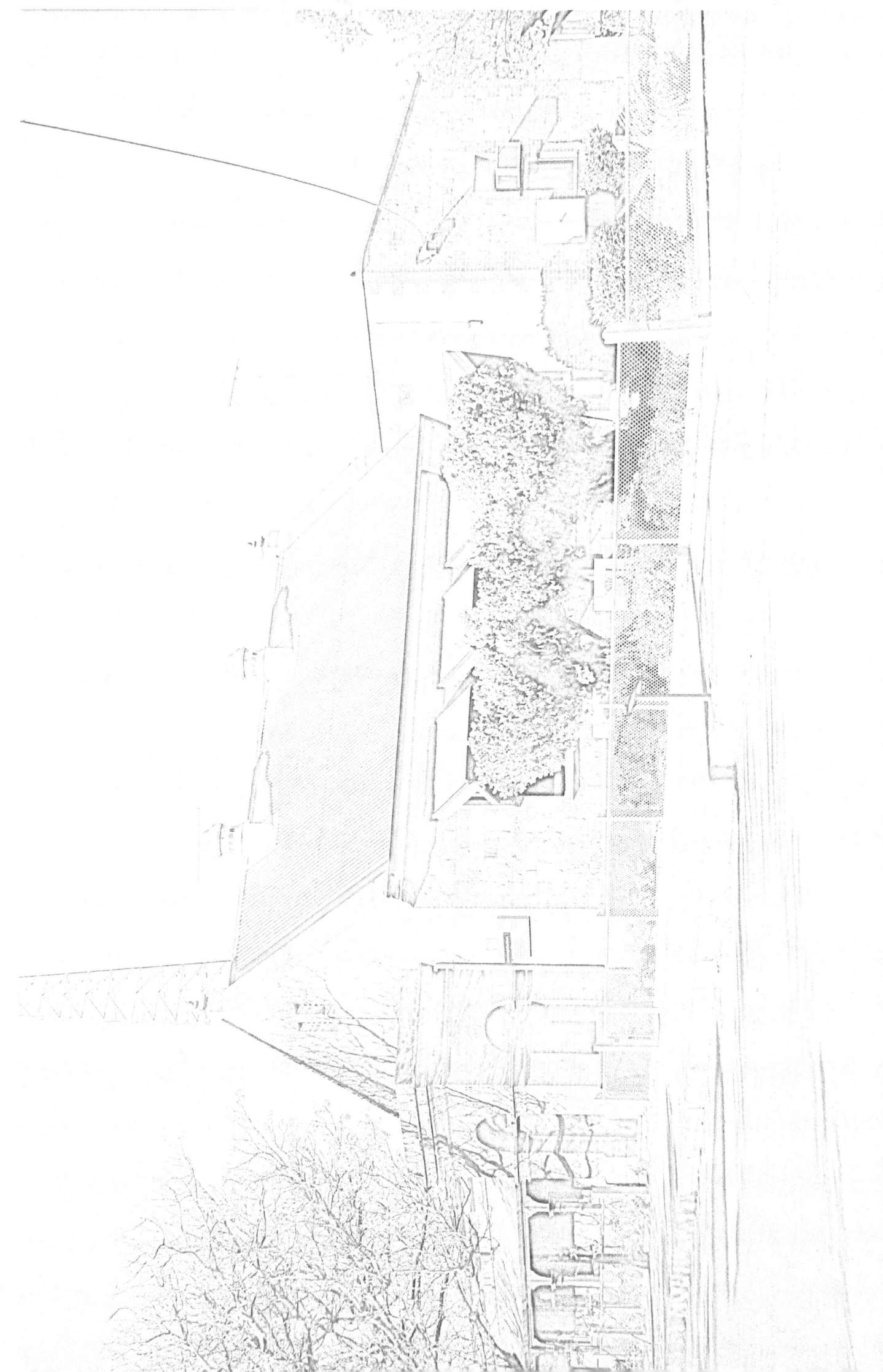

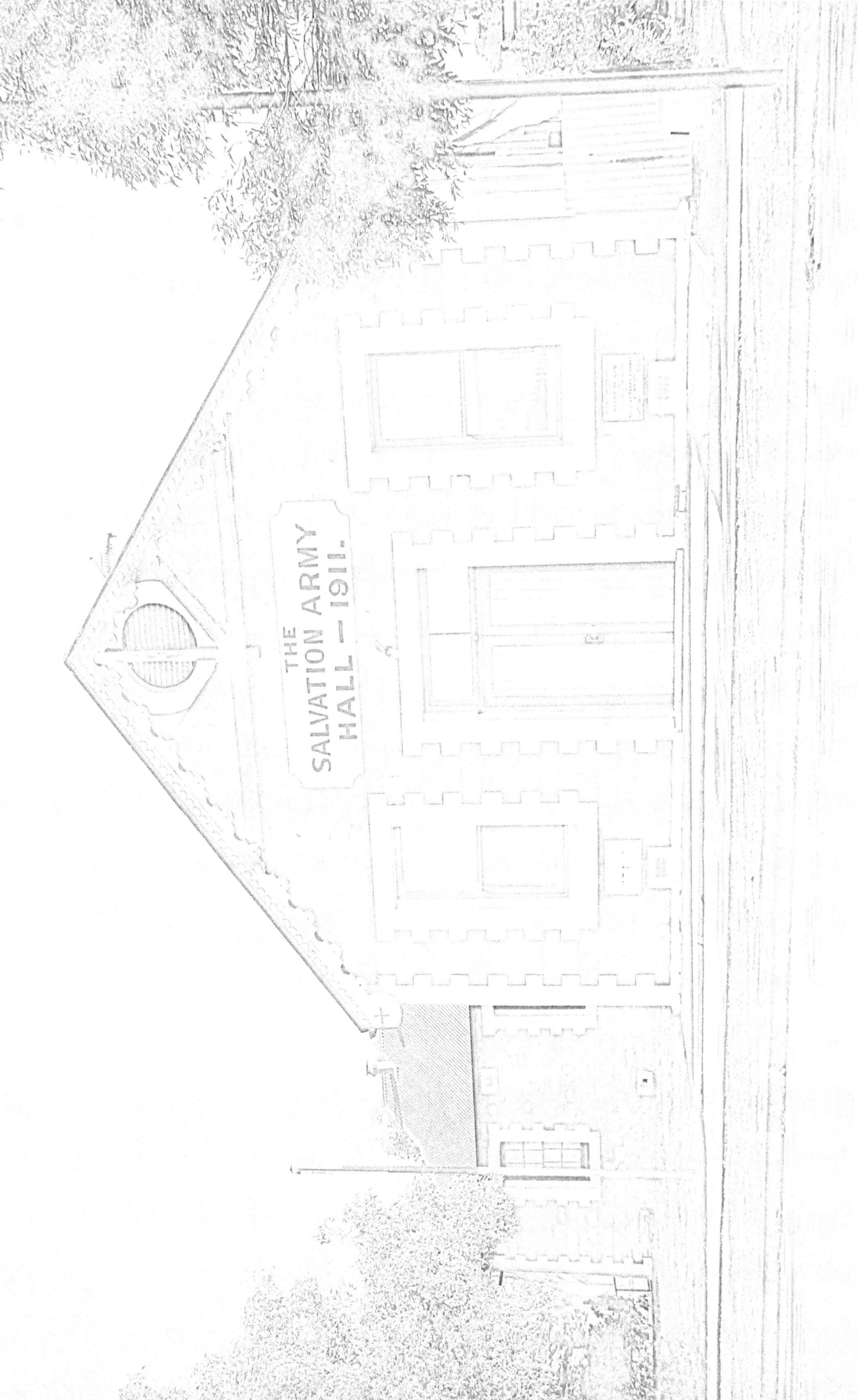

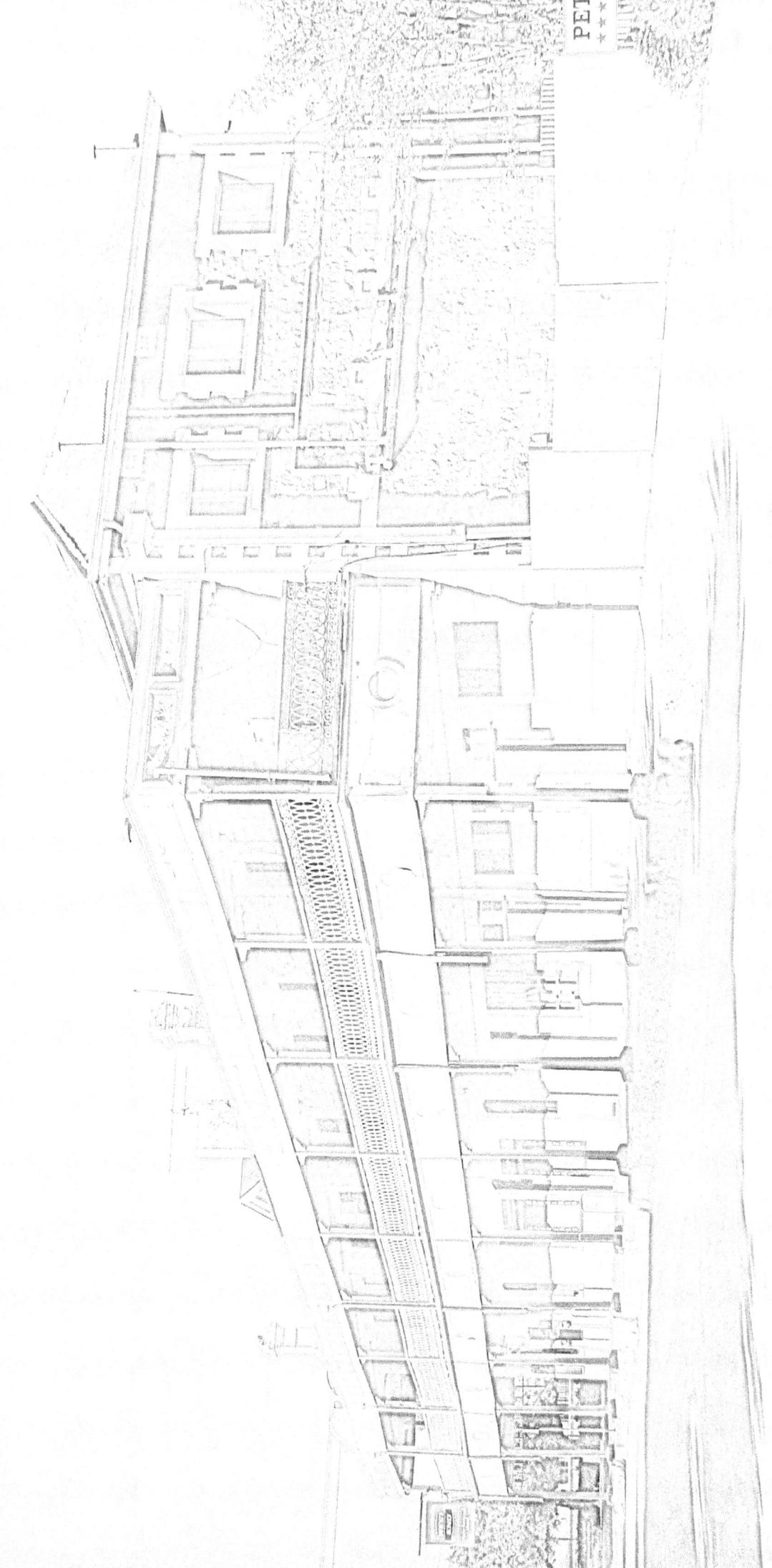

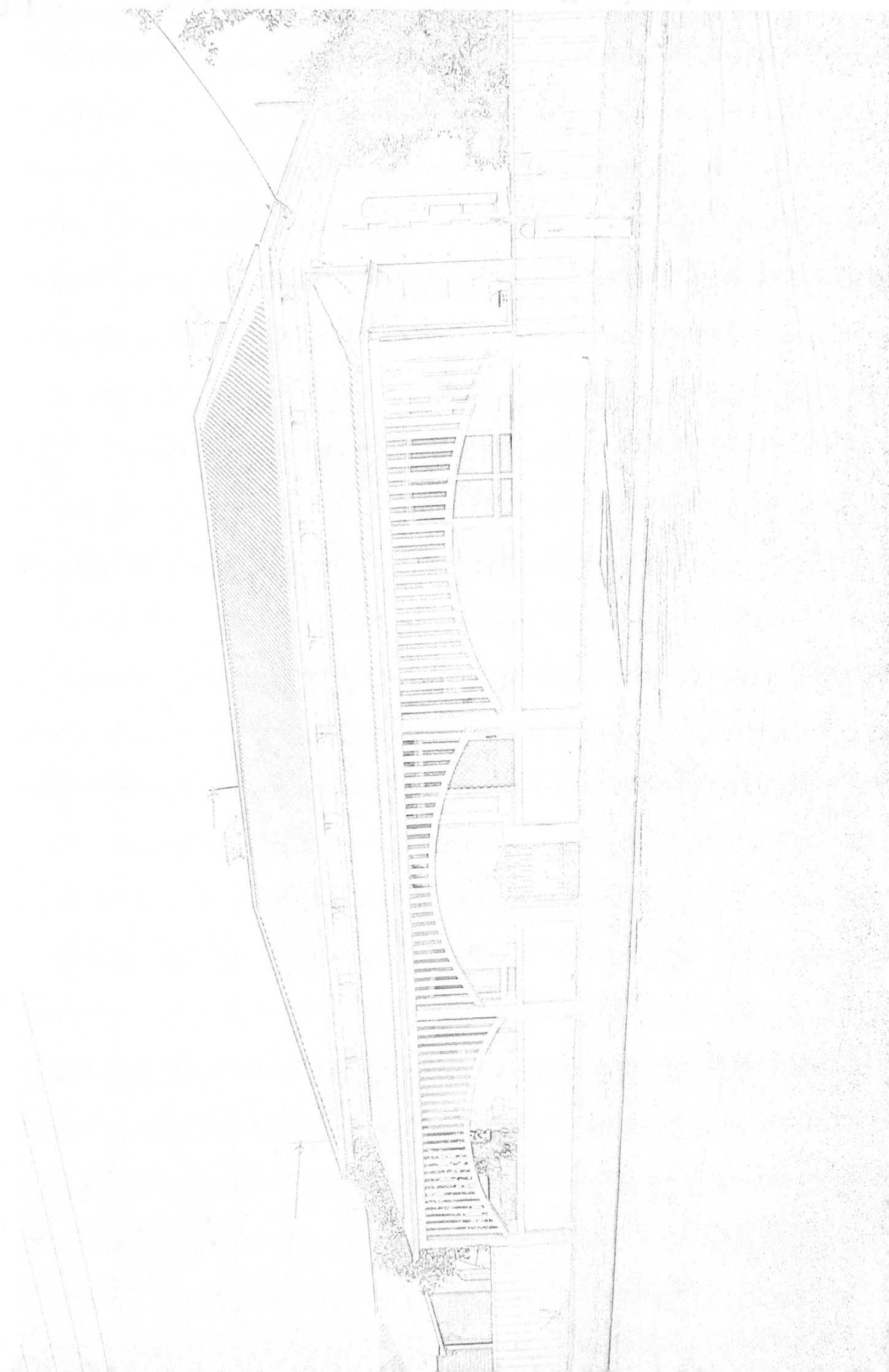

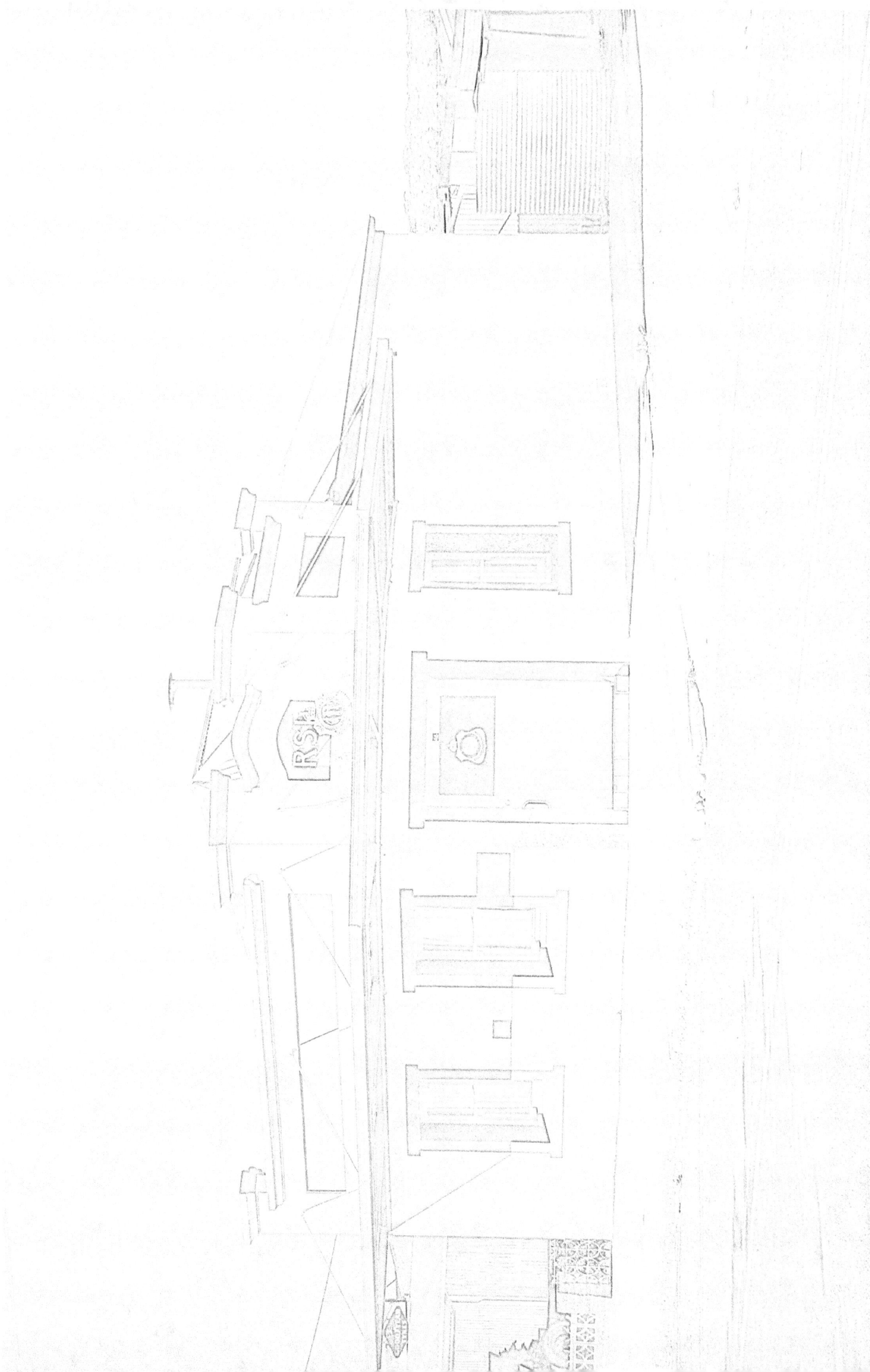

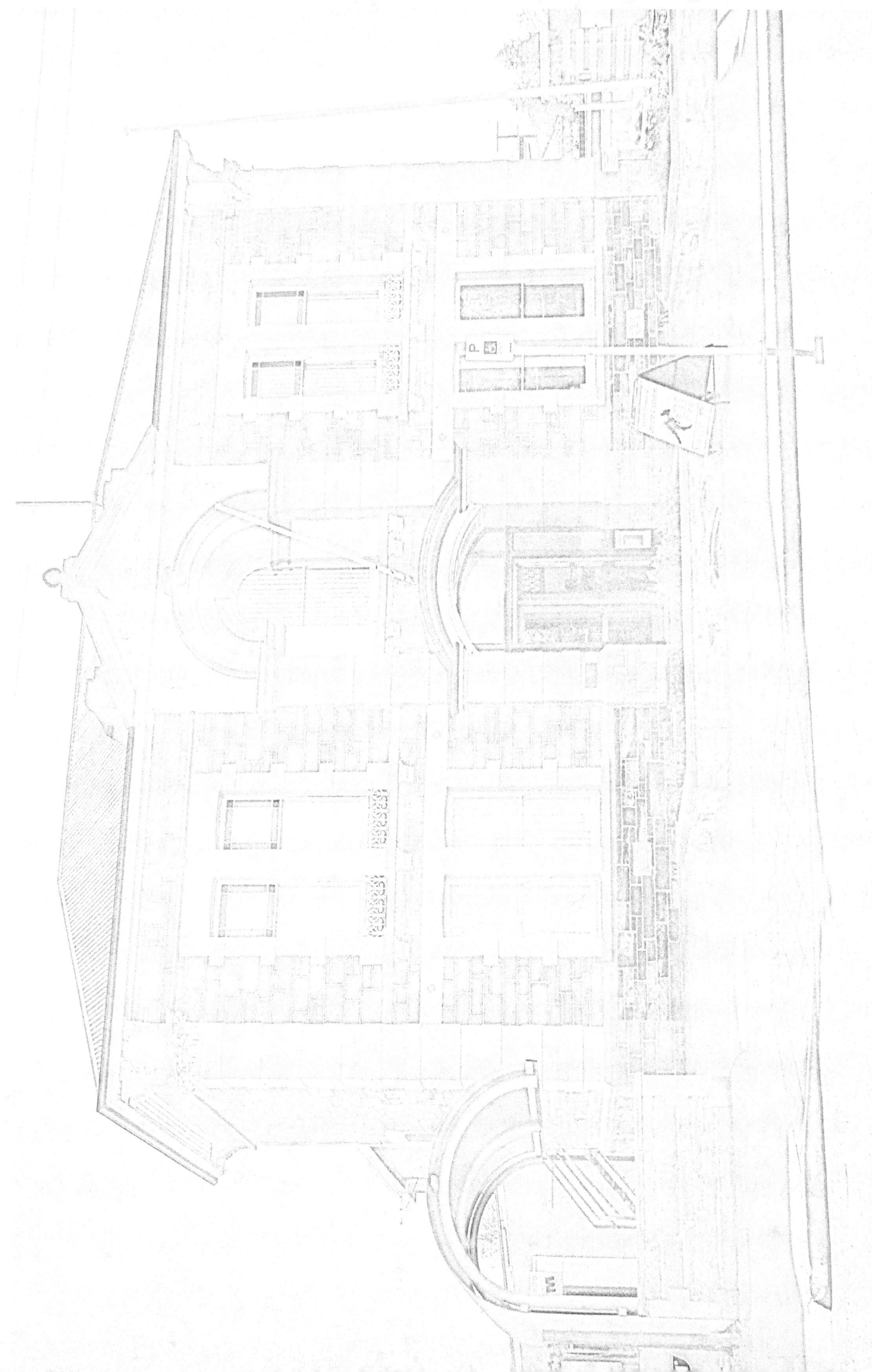

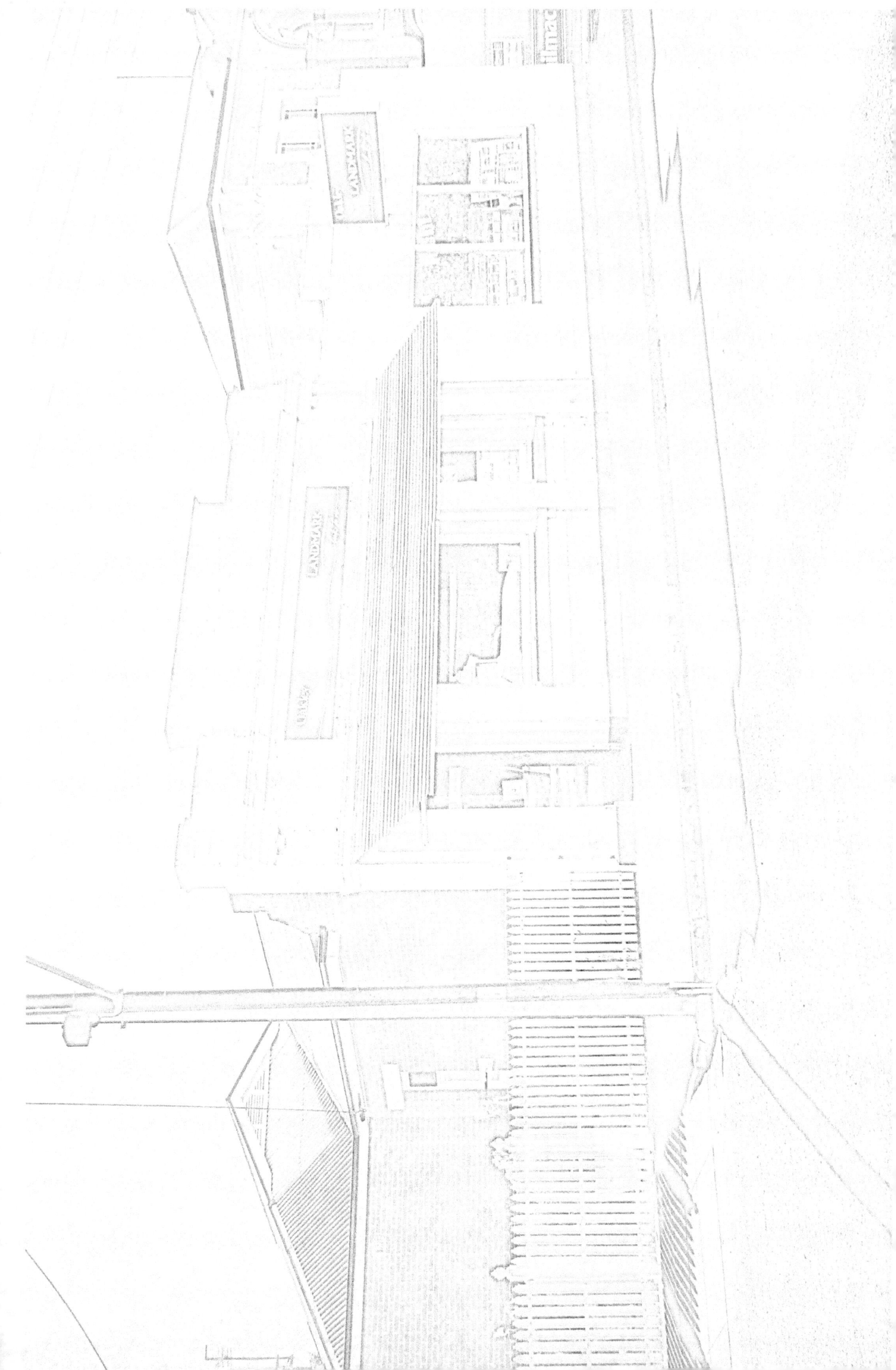

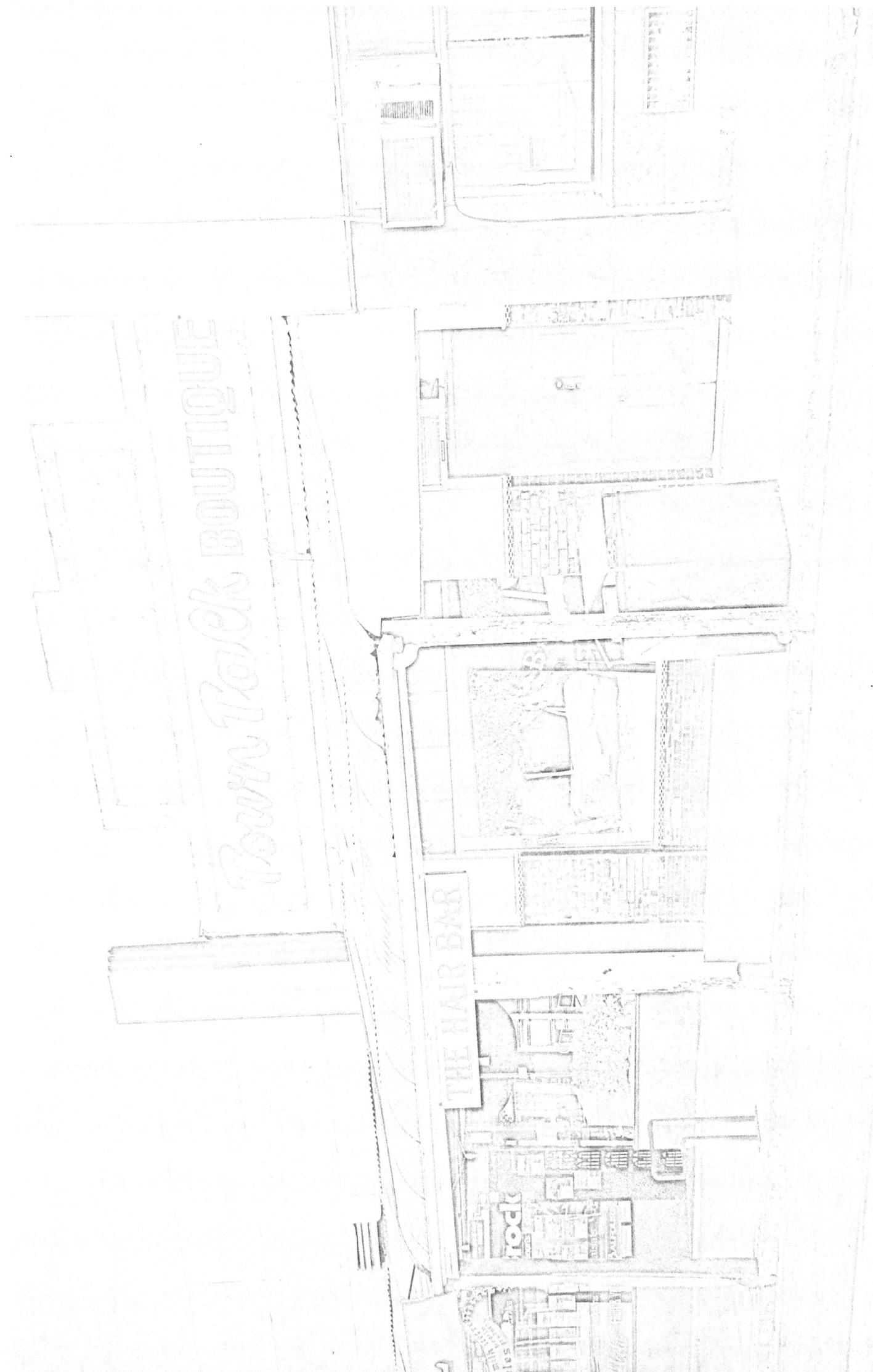

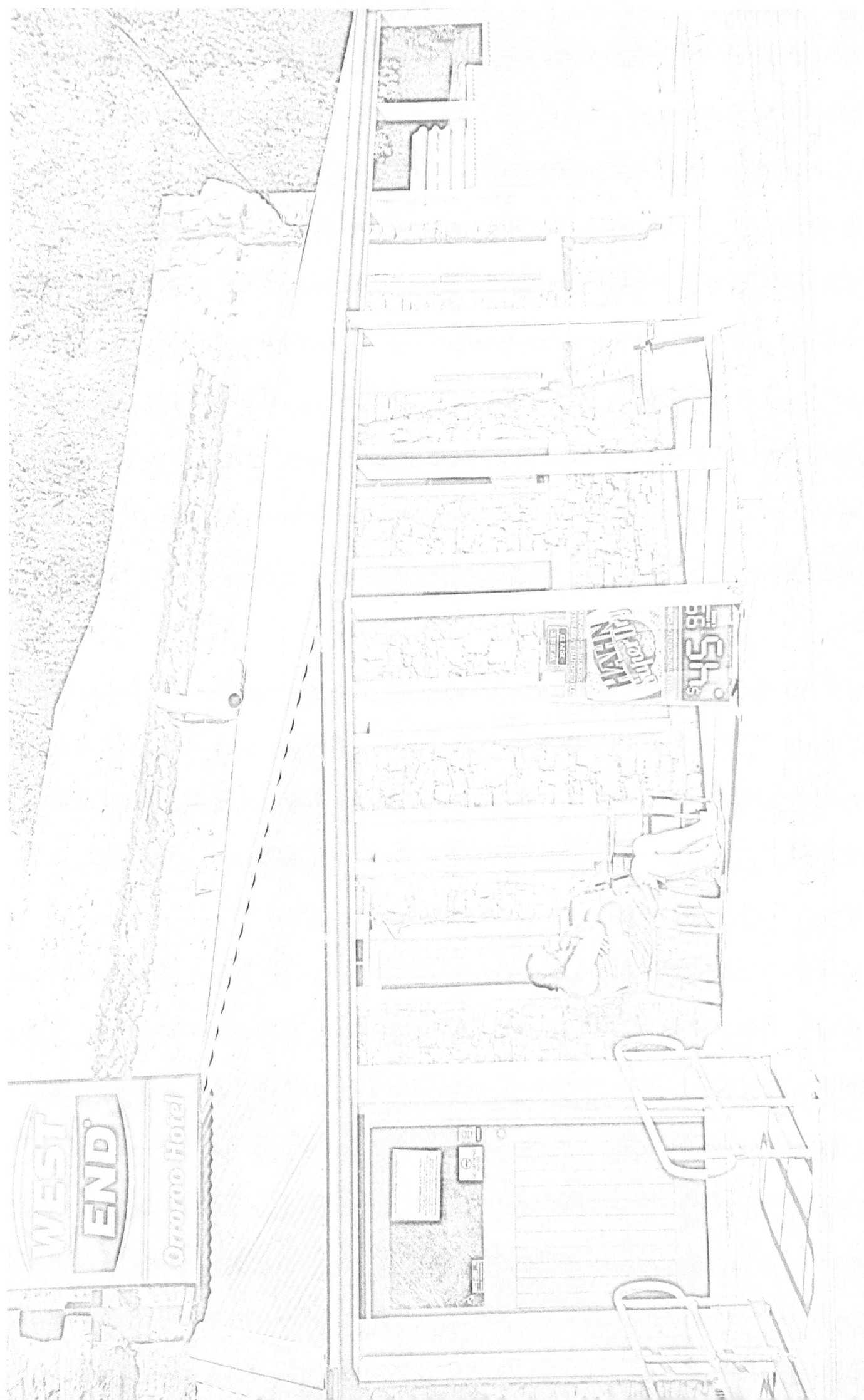

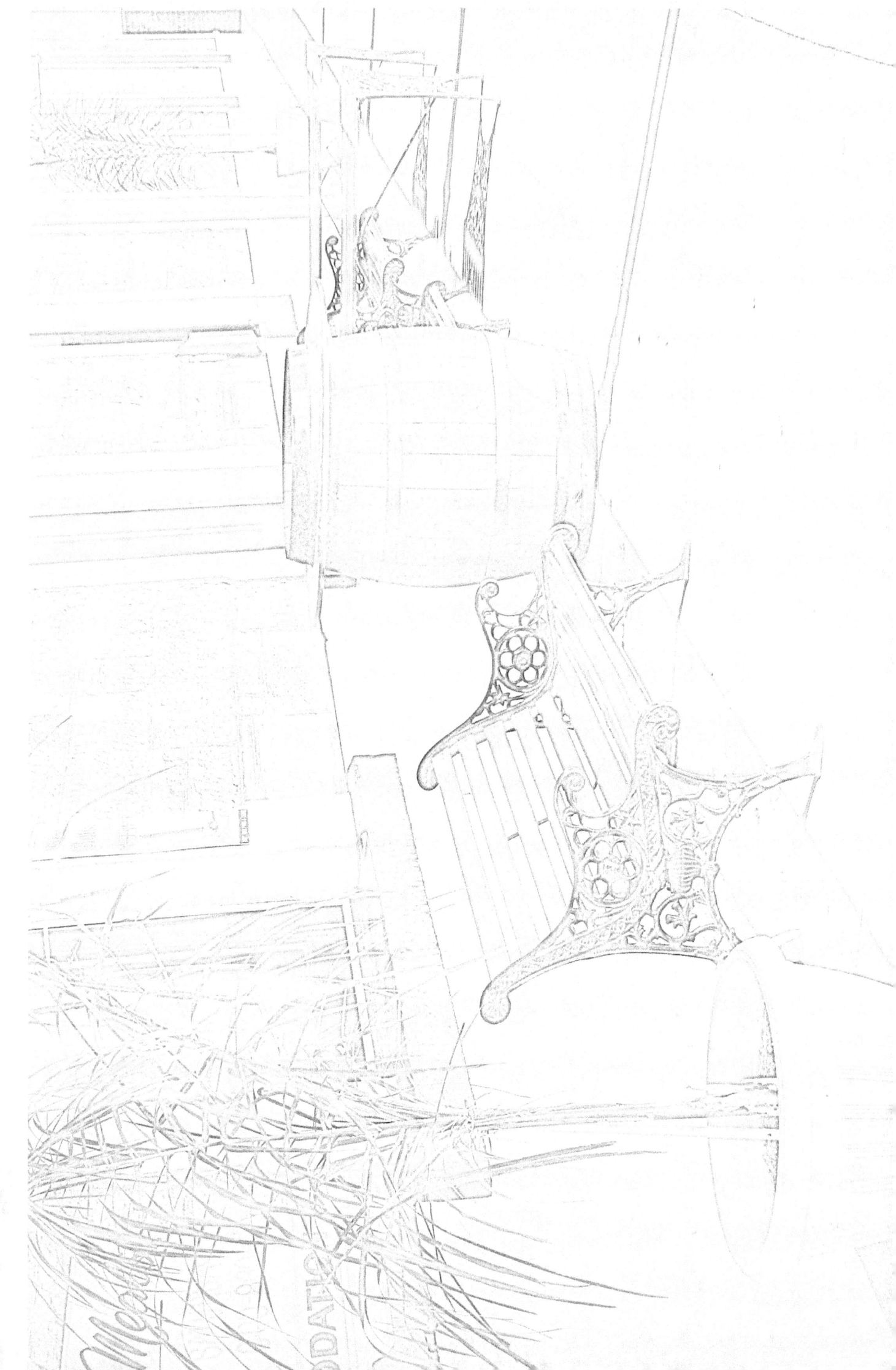